COSTUME of ANCIENT EGYPT

PHILIP J WATSON

drawings by Jack Cassin-Scott

CHELSEA HOUSE PUBLISHERS
NEW YORK · NEW HAVEN · PHILADELPHIA

© Philip J. Watson 1987

First published 1987

Published in the U.S.A. by
Chelsea House Publishers,
a division of
Main Line Book Company

Printed in Great Britain

First Printing

1 3 5 7 9 8 6 4 2

Library of Congress Cataloguing in Publication Data

Watson, Philip J.
  Costume of Ancient Egypt.

  (Costume of the ancient world)
  Bibliography: p.
  Summary: Outlines the geography and history of Ancient
Egypt and describes, in text and illustrations, the
materials and methods used to make clothing and the
typical styles of the era.
  1. Costume—Egypt—History—Juvenile literature.
2. Costume—History—To 500—Juvenile literature.
  [1. Costume—Egypt—History. 2. Costume—History—To
500] I. Cassin-Scott, Jack, ill. II. Title.
GT533.W38 1988   391'.00932   87-15842
  ISBN 1-55546-771-7

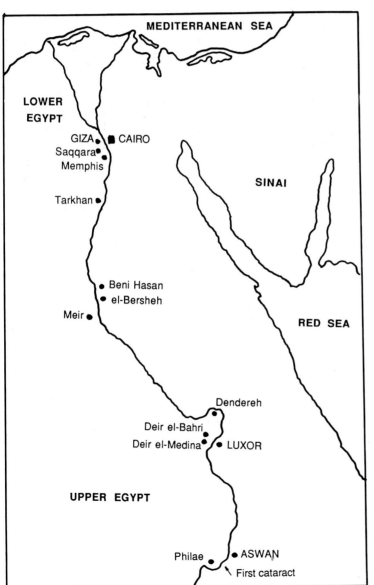

Contents

Chronological table

Note only kings mentioned in the text are listed individually

	BC		BC
Predynastic Period	ends *c* 3100	**New Kingdom**	1570–1070
King Scorpion		*Dynasty XVIII*	1570–1293
		Tuthmosis I	1524–1518
Early Dynastic Period	*c* 3100–2686	Tuthmosis III	1504–1450
Dynasty I	3100–2890	Hatshepsut	1498–1483
King Narmer	3100– ?	Amenophis II	1453–1419
Dynasty II	2890–2686	Tuthmosis IV	1419–1386
Khasekhem	? –2686	Amenophis III	1386–1349
		Amenophis IV	1350–1334
Old Kingdom	2686–2181	(Amarna Period)	
Dynasty III	2686–2613	Tutankhamun	1334–1325
Sekhemkhet	2649–2643	*Dynasty XIX*	1293–1185
Dynasty IV	2613–2498	Rameses II	1279–1212
Dynasty V	2498–2345	*Dynasty XX*	1185–1070
Dynasty VI	2345–2181	Rameses III	1182–1151
First Intermediate Period	2181–2040	**Third Intermediate Period**	1069–525
Dynasties VII – XI		*Dynasties XXI-XXV*	1069–664
		Dynasty XXVI	664–525
Middle Kingdom	2040–1786		
Dynasty XI pt 2	2040–1991	**Late Period**	525–332
Dynasty XII	1991–1786	*Dynasties XXVII-XXX*	
Amenemes I	1991–1962		
		Graeco-Roman Period	332 BC–AD 323
Second Intermediate Period	1786–1570	Alexander the Great	332–323 BC
Dynasties XIII-XVII			

1 Outline of Ancient Egypt

If asked, anyone could say something about Egypt. It has been widely popularized through the pyramids, mummies and Tutankhamun and regularly occurs in news reports about the modern political scene in the Middle East. Let us delve a little more deeply however.

If one consults an atlas it can be seen that modern Egypt (there were of course no such boundaries in ancient times) has an area of some million square kilometres, roughly four times bigger than the UK. Of this vast area however only about 34,000 square kilometres are suitable for agriculture, a mere 3.5% of the total. In other words the habitable area is about one seventh the size of the UK, or slightly larger than Belgium but smaller than Switzerland. The river Nile is about 1200 kilometres long from Aswan in the south to the Mediterranean coast though the maximum width of the Nile valley nowhere exceeds 21 kilometres. For most of its length steep cliffs rise up on either side whilst in the Delta much of the land is swamp. Egyptian agriculture was dependent on the Nile as every year between July and September, depending on locality, it would swell with rainwater running off the Ethiopian highlands and flood the valley floor thereby irrigating the land and depositing a new layer of fine mineral-rich silt (alluvium) washed from the hills.

Egypt was well protected from outsiders by formidable natural barriers. To the east lies desert and mountains all the way to the Red Sea; to the south the Nile is rendered un-navigable by the first cataract; to the west desert stretches virtually uninterrupted all the way to the Atlantic seaboard except for the occasional oasis; to the north the Mediterranean sea presented a threat only from the seafaring peoples of later times. There was a route into Western Asia via Sinai but only the most ambitious, the most organized, or the most desperate attempted the gruelling 160 kilometres of desert.

Climate
There is very little rainfall in Egypt especially south of Cairo, and agriculture depends upon artificial irrigation. In the summer temperatures are extremely high soaring to over 40°C in Aswan; the Delta rarely rises above 30°C. The most pleasant time of year is probably December to March when in Luxor for example the weather would be equivalent to the best of British summers. Evenings do tend to be colder however and temperatures can drop quite sharply after sunset. In late spring, March to

May, sand storms are frequently blown up by south or south westerly winds, the *khamasin.*

History

It is possible to give only the briefest summary of the three thousand years of Egyptian history in a volume of this size. The historical period begins with the unification of the whole of Egypt into a single political unit under the control of one king. The king was Narmer, the date about 3100 BC. It is at this time that Egyptian writing, *hieroglyphic,* first appears, as well as the first monumental architecture. Egyptian rulers are divided into dynasties though these were not used by the Egyptians themselves and were coined by a later historian called Manetho, a native Egyptian writing in Greek. The dynastic system is retained by modern scholars for convenience. The first two dynasties following unification are known as the Early Dynastic period.

Thereafter Egypt's history follows a pattern of classical eras separated by 'dark ages' about which our knowledge is scant. The first of the classical periods is known as the Old Kingdom and comprises dynasties three-six (2686–2181 BC). It was during this time that the great stone pyramids at Giza were built and arts and crafts flourished. After an interval of political breakdown the second of the classical eras, the Middle Kingdom, arose. It is normally taken to run from the latter part of the eleventh dynasty to the end of the twelfth. The period is renowned for its literature, refinement of the arts and increasing contacts with peoples outside the Nile valley. A second dark age was followed by the truly golden age of Egyptian civilization – the New Kingdom (dynasties eighteen–twenty = 1567–1085 BC). The peoples of Nubia in the south were annexed and control was maintained over much of Syria-Palestine. As a result much wealth in the form of war booty and annual tribute accrued to the royal treasury and the temple coffers. The last eight hundred years of Egyptian history before the conquest by Alexander the Great in 332 BC were of mixed fortune. Egypt never regained the glory of the New Kingdom however.

Sources

The evidence from which archaeologists and historians build up a picture of ancient Egypt is derived from several sources. In the case of the present volume the richest body of evidence is the hundreds of paintings and reliefs which have been preserved on the walls of Egyptian tombs. From the earliest periods the Egyptians believed in an afterlife to which one's essential spirit passed after death. It was visualized as being simply a bigger and better version of earthly life where crops were heavier and animals fatter. The paintings and reliefs which decorated the walls of richer tombs from the Old Kingdom onwards acted as a sort of insurance to ensure that this dream, this idealized eternal existence after death, really came true. Fortunately for us they have recorded a wealth of information, textual and pictorial about life in ancient Egypt from which this volume has drawn heavily. It is also worth noting that one of the conditions for eternal existence after death was that one's name should be 'remembered in the mouths of men' and so, perhaps inadvertantly, by studying the ancient tomb scenes we are granting the Egyptians the immortality which they so eagerly craved.

It has already been mentioned that the tomb scenes represent an ideal situation and so it is not surprising to find a certain discrepancy between actual artefacts and the depiction of them. Many objects have been preserved and recovered from tombs where they had been placed as offerings and equipment essential for the deceased's needs and comfort in the afterworld. The funerary statues, like the wall scenes, reflect an idealized viewpoint whilst the more usable items of funerary furniture often seem to have been examples taken from everyday life, sometimes even showing signs of wear and use. The discrepancy between the depictions and reality varies depending on the category of object. Unfortunately for us the examples of real garments found in the tombs only partially correspond to the scenes and the gap between the two sources is at times difficult to bridge. Proportionally speaking relatively few real garments have survived compared to the number depicted in painting, relief and statuary and this imbalance is necessarily transmitted in the following pages. The reader should bear in mind that the tomb scenes reflect the equivalent of one's best suit whilst the material remains comprise more the denims and boiler suits. For those wishing to reconstruct Egyptian costumes a judicious combination of the simple yet effective techniques of the surviving garments with the comparative elegance and variety found in the tomb scenes should not fall too short of the mark.

The vast body of written evidence from ancient Egypt, whilst of primary importance for reconstructing our knowledge of the Egyptian textile industry, relative prices and so on is of little value for re-creating the garments themselves.

2 Materials and methods

Before examining Egyptian costume itself it is pertinent to give a brief survey of the materials which were available to the ancient Egyptian dressmaker and the techniques which had been developed to treat and finish them.

Fibres

The two basic raw materials from which cloth could be made were flax and wool. Flax, from which linen is made, was cultivated in ancient Egypt at a very early period, certainly from 5000 BC onwards. The flax seeds were sown in mid-November and pulled about four months later. The tomb scenes allow us to follow the processes used in the preparation of flax which was very similar to the methods used in Ireland until recent times. After pulling, the stems were sorted into sizes and bound in stooks to dry. When dry they were *rippled* using a large wooden comb with long teeth to remove any bolls and other extraneous matter. The next process, *retting*, involved soaking the stems in water for about fifteen days to soften the woody parts which, after drying out, were removed by beating the stems with a wooden mallet or blade. Any remaining wood and short or broken fibres were then removed by a final combing; waste fibres were used as lamp wicks. The stems were harvested at different stages of ripeness depending on the eventual use. The finest threads came from young green stems; older yellow stems produced fibres suitable for good quality linen whilst the fully mature plants were more suited to rope and mat making.

Both sheep and goats were kept in Egypt and it is obvious that wool was used to make warm clothing and blankets despite the statement by the Greek historian Herodotus that it was considered ritually unclean. Certainly there is abundant evidence for the spinning of wool and it was probably much more widely used than has often been supposed, especially for domestic purposes.

Although there is evidence that certain species of grass and hemp were used to produce woven fabrics, this was not usual. Other materials such as cotton and silk were not introduced into Egypt until post-pharaonic times.

Spinning

The most primitive method of spinning either flax or wool is simple hand spinning in which the fibres are rolled between the palms of the hands or between palm and thigh. Slightly more advanced is the grasped spindle technique in which the threads are drawn over a forked stick to a spindle, usually a short stick or trimmed twig, which was rotated between both hands. Equally primitive is the supported spindle method. Here the thread is guided by hand onto the spindle which is then rotated against the thigh. All of these methods produce coarse and uneven yarns.

A more sophisticated technique capable of producing very fine threads of even quality is known as suspended spindle. In this method the thread is drawn through the fingers onto a spindle which is spun and dropped allowing it to swing. A small weight, called a whorl, was attached to the spindle to maintain the spin once it had been dropped.

Egyptian spindles up to the Middle Kingdom have a deep spiral groove at the top whilst in the New Kingdom examples are hooked. Whorls were usually made from wood, pottery or stone but mud, bone and other materials are found. Middle Kingdom whorls are cylindrical with flat tops and bases; New Kingdom examples have flat bases but convex, domed tops. It was normal practice in Egypt to attach the whorl near the top of the spindle.

In flax spinning the prepared dried fibres, or 'roves' were wound into balls on pottery spools and placed in pots containing pierced lids which guided the threads smoothly to the spindle. Flax was spun anticlockwise (s-spun) and this is the direction in which flax fibres naturally rotate. Plyed yarns comprising two or more threads were made by spinning the requisite number of threads together in the opposite direction.

Dyeing

Both wool and flax were normally dyed before weaving except in the case of white fabrics where the finished cloth was bleached. Bleaching simply consisted of exposing the materials to the strong Egyptian sunlight. It was necessary to wash both wool and flax before dyeing them normally with one of the natural detergents available to the Egyptians. These comprised natron (basically soda), potash and a variety of alkaline plants. Hot aqueous solutions of dyes, usually extracted from plants, were used. Red was obtained from madder roots and more rarely henna, yellow from safflower and blue from indigotin, a form of woad, and the seed pods of certain acacia bushes. Intermediate colours could be obtained by double dyeing; for example indigo and safflower produces green, indigo and madder purple and so on. A mordant, possibly alum from the western oases was used to fix the colours.

Weaving

The art of weaving is normally assumed to have arisen out of basketry and certainly this industry was of primary importance in Egypt. The earliest buildings in the predynastic periods were made out of reed bundle frameworks covered over with reed mats. Throughout Egyptian history basketry was in constant and common use for production of baskets, mats, hurdles, sandals and many other items.

Before weaving begins the warp, those fibres which run the length of the fabric, has to be laid down. The Egyptian sources record three methods of warping. Primitive but effective in a frameless loom is the practice of simply winding the required number of threads round the beams of the loom; this method is still used by present-day nomads in parts of the Middle East. Alternatively the warp threads are wound in a figure of eight onto pegs set into a wall and then transferred to the loom separately. Another method shows warping around three or four pegs hammered into the ground (figure 1. See colour plate 1).

Doubtless the Egyptians used the various makeshift and primitive looms which can still be found today though the sources record two main types. The earlier is the horizontal ground loom (figure 1). This is a frameless loom consisting of two beams, between which is stretched the warp, supported on four low posts set into the ground. During the New Kingdom a vertical framed loom was introduced, probably from Syria (figure 2). In this the two beams carrying the warp were set in a rectangular wooden frame. The vertical loom did not displace the horizontal though it did allow new techniques, such as tapestry and pattern weaving, to be carried out. It would appear that horizontal looms were normally operated by women whilst vertical looms were a man's domain.

Fabrics
The earliest fabrics were simple, plain weaves but with time quite complex variations were introduced. As already mentioned, pattern and tapestry weaves are encountered from the New Kingdom onwards. Looped techniques produced fabrics with a pile for towels whilst in others the pile is tufted. Selvedges and warp ends were often left as fringes. The texture of linen could vary from the finest, translucent gauzes to quite coarse canvas. The Egyptians themselves distinguished various grades such as royal linen, byssus, fine cloth, ordinary cloth and so on.

Making Up
The practices of sewing and darning are attested both by examples of the equipment used and from examination of surviving garments. Needles, made variously of bronze, bone, wood and other materials, pins, reels and bobbins survive in large quantities. Various methods of sewing seams and hems are known though normally they were simply rolled over and held by a series of whipped stitches. Embroidery was not an Egyptian technique though garments were often decorated with applied beads. Repairs were effected by darning in the earlier periods; surprisingly patching was not introduced until the later phases of Egyptian history when it replaced darning.

Leather
It is not intended here to give a detailed description of leather-working and tanning. However it should be noted that hides of both domesticated and wild animals such as gazelles and leopards were used in the manufacture

2   New Kingdom vertical loom

of clothing and accessories. Loincloths, sandals, shoes and rarely gloves are amongst the products for which leather was used as well as equipment such as shields and quivers.

Organization of textile industry

It is obvious that spinning and weaving and presumably also therefore sewing and manufacture of garments took place at all levels of Egyptian society. The ladies of the royal harem attached to the palace are known to have supervised weavers whilst most of the larger temples had textile workshops under their control. These latter would have produced fabrics and garments for use in the temple and clothing the statue of the god. Doubtless a surplus would have been produced with which to barter for other commodities or to add to the coffers in the temple treasury. The deity's garments would have been made from the finest quality 'royal linen'. Funerary models and tomb scenes show weaving and spinning operations on a medium scale (two operational looms) taking place on the estates of the nobles and higher officials whilst there is evidence to suggest a thriving cottage industry amongst peasant families producing textiles both for home consumption and barter as a means of supplementing the family income. The tomb scenes depict men, women and children alike all playing a part in these very necessary activities.

3 Nobles and officials

The higher officials, or *nobles* as they are often called, are the most frequently encountered people in ancient Egyptian art both in tomb scenes and sculpture. They represent the upper echelons of Egyptian society immediately below the king and the royal circle though in close contact with the court. They formed what in our modern terms would be the civil service, the judiciary, local government officials, higher military leaders and higher churchmen. They included officials such as *vizier* (the chief minister or Lord Chancellor), overseer of the treasury, of the granary, of the army, scribes, high priests of various gods, and so on.

The common dress of men of these ranks, indeed the men's garment found most often in ancient Egypt on any class and at any period, was the kilt or wrap-around skirt. It could vary in quality of material, length, style of cut and decoration as we shall see but remained basically the same garment in concept – namely a rectangular length of cloth wrapped around the hips with one end overlapping the other. It was secured either by simply tucking the outer end into the tightly wrapped 'waist', tucking it into a belt or by a tie of some sort.

Old Kingdom

Numerous examples of the simple kilt can be seen in the tomb scenes and funerary statues of the Old Kingdom. The characteristic pose for the latter throughout the Old Kingdom depicts the man standing with one leg forward in a striding posture normally holding a staff in one hand and a sceptre in the other. Exceptionally, scribes are shown seated cross-legged writing on or reading from a roll of papyrus. The so-called short kilt normally ends just above the knees and was made from a suitable grade of linen bleached white. Coloured examples are rarely encountered.

Most usually the kilts of the noble classes had the overlapping end tailored to a curve which was then pleated vertically (figure 3). On private statues kilts are shown wrapped so that the curved overlap falls on the right. The kilt was supported by a linen belt fastened with an ingenious double loop and the overlapping section was held firm by a rectangular tab which is usually shown projecting up from behind the belt rather like the hilt of a dagger.

More elaborately treated versions had the curved overlap crimped in a series of wavy pleats. Such a garment is worn by an official of the third dynasty, Hesy-Re, whose tomb was decorated with beautifully carved

3   Old Kingdom official wearing a kilt with pleated overlap

wooden panels. Conversely and less frequent are kilts with tailored, curved overlaps not pleated, but finished with a fringe (figure 4).

A slightly longer version of the kilt which ended just below the knees was often starched at the front so that the bottom hem projected forwards (figure 5). Such kilts were usually unpleated and untailored. They finish with a straight edge and are normally simply secured by tucking them into the belt or waistband. Instances are known of funerary statues depicting the same person in both this kilt and the shorter one with curved pleated overlap suggesting that there was perhaps some distinction of usage or occasion between the two.

Not infrequently this longer kilt was tailored and starched to create a flaring triangular apron at the front, a rather ridiculous looking garment which must surely have been impractical for everyday use (figure 6). However, such kilts are depicted with considerable frequency. Scribes are often shown seated with a papyrus on the lap of their kilt which was perhaps starched to give it rigidity. As all nobles and officials would have been schooled and were therefore scribes it is possible that this kilt represents specifically scribal attire. The kilt with starched front is also shown in a much longer version reaching half way down the shins or even almost to the ankles but never actually to them. The starched fronts must have been particularly cumbersome in these examples (figure 7).

The torso is always naked in the Old Kingdom though the neck is sometimes adorned with a simple necklace or collar. On some a scarf-like garment is shown. The example seen in figure 7 is green and white striped and is wrapped once around the front of the neck, passes round the back and the two ends are thrown over onto the front of the chest where they hang. There is a single tassel on each end. A similar scarf described as a stole but worn in a slightly different fashion is seen on an otherwise naked figure leading bulls in the tomb of Ptahhetep at Saqqara.

A first dynasty mastaba tomb at Tarkhan yielded a noble's garment which showed signs of having been worn during the owner's lifetime. This consisted of a high-waisted skirt made from a single piece of material 76 cm wide joined selvedge to selvedge down the left side with whipping stitches. There was an ornamental weft fringe. The upper part of the garment consisted of sleeves and yoke cut from two pieces of material which were sewn to the skirt meeting to form a V-shaped neckline at both front and back. The sleeves and the yoke were done with tight accordion pleats which followed the line of the shoulders down the arms.

Middle Kingdom

The nobles and officials of the Middle Kingdom continued to wear kilts which followed Old Kingdom fashions. Thus one continues to encounter in Middle Kingdom art the short kilt tailored into a curved overlap, either left plain or pleated, as well as the kilt with a starched apron at the front, both the short and long versions.

A slightly different type of kilt, or perhaps merely a different mode of wearing the plain kilt, appears in the Middle Kingdom. It occurs in varying

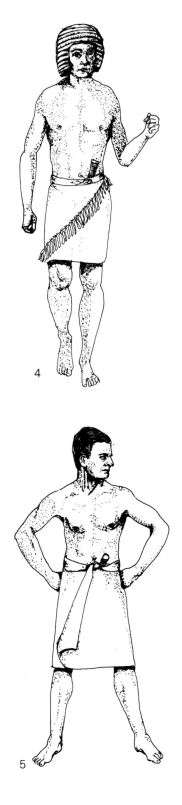

4

5

12

lengths but is always 'midi', that is below the knees but above the ankles. It hangs so as to leave two triangles of cloth, points downward, protruding beyond the hem line. The upper edge of the material is usually fringed but otherwise the garments are plain (figure 8).

The tripartite *shendyt* (see page 28) was almost exclusively reserved for use by the king in the Old Kingdom though it is not uncommonly seen on officials of the Middle Kingdom. Although usually made of plain linen examples can be found of private individuals wearing *shendyt*-kilts with pleating all over as was customary for royalty in the Old Kingdom.

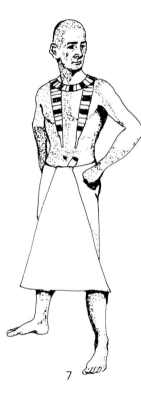

6

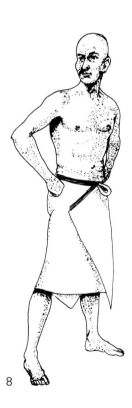

7

8

4   Old Kingdom kilt with fringed edge

5   The longer version of the Old Kingdom kilt

6   Kilt with starched triangular apron at the front

7   A long kilt with starched apron

8   See colour plate 3

13

There is more evidence from the Middle Kingdom of garments being worn in combination. Figure 9 for example shows a noble, a local governor, wearing a plain *shendyt*-kilt over which is worn a long, calf-length skirt, pleated, and with a starched apron at the front. It is likely that this longer overskirt was made of much finer possibly semi-transparent material. Another 'suit' is shown in figure 10 where a much simpler, knee-length kilt is worn again in conjunction with a longer overskirt but likewise plain. Round his shoulders there is thrown a cape-like shawl which covers the shoulders, upper arms and most of the chest. It is secured by knotting or pinning the two ends where they meet, roughly over the stomach.

This is a rare example of a garment for the upper body. Generally in the Middle Kingdom the usual practice was, as in the Old Kingdom, to leave the torso bare. The scarf or sash which was encountered above however is still found though what functional purpose this might have served is conjectural. Most of the examples known from the Middle Kingdom have pointed ends, not square or tasselled, and can be either plain or striped. They are donned by officials, priests offering incense and attendants bringing in offerings for inspection.

A scene in a rock tomb at Meir showing a twelfth dynasty nomarch named Senbi and his son hunting gazelle and other game in the desert preserves some interesting details of costume (figure 11).

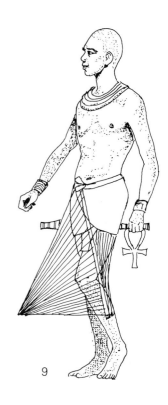

9

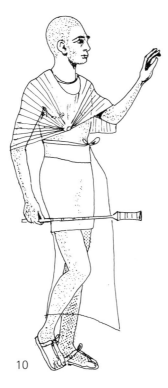

10

9   Official wearing a long pleated skirt over a *shendyt*-kilt

10   Middle Kingdom noble in short kilt, overshirt and cape

Both wear a type of back apron reaching to just below their knees similar to those worn by archers. Senbi's is supported by a tightly-bound cloth or leather girdle wrapped four times round the waist and then tied in a knot. The knot perhaps indicates cloth but on the basis of modern parallels leather has been suggested. The son's is held by a simple belt or waistband.

Both have a penis-sheath consisting of a narrow tube and a 'sporran'-like flap. The penis is inserted in the tube the mouth of which is tied. The tube and sporran are then passed through the belt so that the penis is held up whilst the wider flap hangs down to cover the front of the body thereby providing both decency and protection. The tomb scenes indicate that similar garments were worn by soldiers. Senbi carries a bow and spare arrows and has an X-shaped sash across his chest, probably straps to hold a quiver in place on his back.

His son has an ostrich feather in his hair and on his shoulder carries a goat skin bag, possibly a water bottle. He is well armed with a dagger tucked into his belt, an axe and a quiver full of arrows. Both men are barefoot.

11   Middle Kingdom hunting costume, also worn by soldiers

What appears to be a new introduction in the Middle Kingdom is a skirt which wraps around the body from the back and is held up by tabs which tuck into the tightly wrapped overfold (figure 12). These skirts are always high waisted, sometimes extending almost to the bottom of the breasts and are usually long, reaching to the mid-calves. Exceptionally one instance occurs of such a high waisted skirt which ends at the knees though a longer over garment is worn in conjunction with it apparently draped from the same point. The waistband can be either plain or fringed and although most examples are plain some are found with a horizontal striped pattern or with pleats.

A similar garment, equally characteristic of the Middle Kingdom, consists purely of a rectangular blanket which is simply wrapped, hardly draped, around the body. Versions are made from both plain and horizontally striped material; on one of the latter the stripes are coloured with stippled green dots. The stippling is more intense at the top of the stripe gradually becoming less dense towards the lower edge of the stripe which is left plain white. This gradual fading of the colour gives a shaded effect suggesting a flounced garment rather than a flat piece of cloth. It is often asserted that these blanket robes were made of wool and were worn for warmth at night or when it was cold, and parallels for this can be seen in the practices of the modern fellahin. Certainly the depictions do suggest a somewhat thicker cloth than the fine linen of the kilts and a scene showing a servant carrying one of these striped blankets over his arm supports this observation; the piece is considerably larger than the bolts of linen which are commonly seen. Some have fringes at the top edge and it has been asserted that these may therefore be made from linen, but there is no reason why a fringe could not be left on a woollen fabric. These garments were worn either draped over both shoulders or over only one. In the former case movement was obviously very restricted and effectively only the hands were free and only one arm had any degree of movement (figure 13). This fashion was more common for women however (figure 32) and men usually wore the blanket over one shoulder only, in most instances the left, leaving the right arm and hand entirely free (figure 14). On one example the skirt of another, longer garment projects below the hem of the woollen blanket; the blanket is coloured in green and white stripes with a red white and green border whilst the underskirt is grey except where it passes over the legs which are clearly indicated suggesting that the underskirt was transparent and therefore of very fine linen.

Very few actual clothes have survived from the Middle Kingdom. Though textile remains are not uncommon they mostly take the form of sheets or bolts of plain cloth many of which were probably used as bed linen though some could have been destined for garment manufacture. Smaller pieces of fringed cloth have been interpreted as kilt cloths and one surviving example had been dyed red. The tomb of Meket-Re which produced a mass of marvellous detailed models illustrating many aspects of daily life (such as the weaving workshop shown in figure 1) also yielded a sleeveless shirt. This consisted merely of a simple rectangle of linen, of

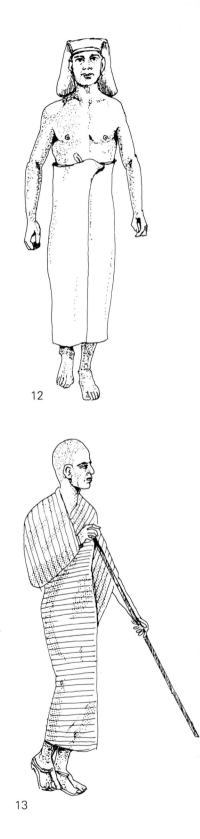

12

13

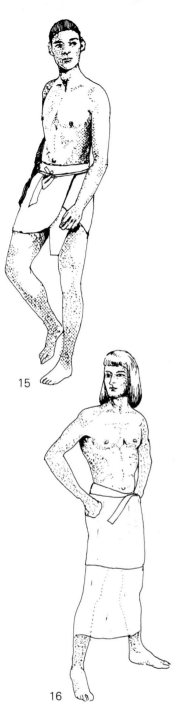

15

16

a fairly fine quality, 142 cm long and 78 cm wide. It had been folded lengthways and sewn together up the sides leaving holes near the top for the arms. Another hole was cut out of the top for the head and neck. The edges of the neck and the hem had been rolled over and sewn with whipping stitches. Another tomb preserved three aprons, never finished, made of soft leather which had been dyed different colours – reddish-brown, black and green.

New Kingdom

During the New Kingdom, seemingly from the reign of Tuthmosis I onwards, there is a marked change in Egyptian fashion for the nobility, at least as depicted in the wall paintings and in sculpture. The relatively severe and somewhat plain, though not necessarily inelegant styles of the earlier periods are replaced by clothes with much more fullness and more elaborate pleating coupled with more imaginative ways of cutting and draping them. However, relatively few actual examples of clothing have survived and those that are known from the New Kingdom exhibit fairly simple, unpretentious patterns and are of mediocre fabric. At this juncture therefore it is necessary to repeat the warning given in the introduction that the monuments depict and reflect very much ideal fashions, one's best suit of clothes as it were, whilst the archaeological record tends to preserve the coarser more durable garments and the gap between these two is not easy to bridge. Also it should be kept in mind that large, sheet-like pieces of cloth are often preserved in tombs and it is likely that many of the fashions in the tomb scenes which show elaborate folds and flaps of material are in fact composed of a simple square or rectangle of material folded, wrapped, draped and tied in various ingenious ways somewhat parallel to an Indian sari. Certainly many of the specifically New Kingdom fashions display an elaborateness, almost frivolity, bordering on the cumbersome, rendering the garments impractical for all but the most ceremonial of occasions.

The standard male garment remains the plain kilt almost always in the New Kingdom ending just above the knee and with the outer, overlapping edge shaped so as better to fit the contour of the leg. Also found is the shorter kilt very similar in appearance to the *shendyt*-kilt (see page 28) but having a narrow, sharply pointed flap at the front rather than the broad, straight-edged flap of the *shendyt* (figure 15). Middle officials, shown supervising workmen, inspecting goods, or recording produce for example, often wear a longer overskirt above the kilt (figure 16). The

12   High waisted Middle Kingdom skirt held up by 'tabs' tucked into the overfold

13   The 'blanket' robe, usually made of wool, here worn draped over both shoulders

14   See colour plate 3

15   A short New Kingdom kilt

16   A middle official wearing kilt and overskirt

paintings usually colour the overskirt white where it passes between the legs but grey or brownish where it actually lies over the top suggesting the shadow of the legs beneath. From this it may be inferred that the overskirts were of a thinner, finer and more diaphanous material than the kilts. Such overskirts appear to have little practical value either for keeping a person warm or for modesty and it is possible that they were worn as much to distinguish non-manual workers from labourers than out of any practical necessity. The length of these overskirts varies but is generally mid-calf length with the hem usually falling somewhere in the middle third of the lower leg. Where variations in length occur in the same scene the more important personage wears the longer overskirt. Hemlines are usually straight but occasionally curve lower towards the front.

In other instances a long tunic with short sleeves was worn over the kilt or even a briefer type of loincloth. This was usually pulled in at the waist by a cord or belt and has a keyhole-shaped neckline fastened with ties. In length the tunics vary from knee- to mid-calf length, rarely lower, and can have straight or concave hemlines. Occasionally tunics were worn over both a kilt and an overskirt (figure 17). In one example (figure 18) the knee-length tunic has a deep inverted 'V' shape cut out of the bottom edge and the loincloth is, rather unusually, worn over the top of it. The loincloth is wrapped several times around the body and a long thin tapering flap hangs down the inside. Its bottom edge is shown as if gathered or scalloped. Similar indication of gathering is found on the bottom of a thigh-length tunic which is pulled in by a tied belt (figure 19). Under it is worn a brief loincloth and long overskirt with fringed hem.

Elaborately draped kilts or wrap-round skirts with all over pleating and sagging waistlines at the front are found in the later New Kingdom (figure 20). The calf-length example illustrated here is vertically pleated but is draped to produce two curving segments falling away from the waist to the sides of the legs with a short, narrow flap of material falling down the front behind them rather as on a *shendyt*-kilt. The end of this flap is decorated with tassels. The garment is so wrapped as to produce a concave waistline at the front whilst rising quite high up the back. This type of kilt was especially popular in the nineteenth dynasty, and doubtless derives stylistically from the royal fashions of the Amarna period in vogue towards the end of the eighteenth dynasty.

Closely related stylistically to these all-over pleated kilts is a garment which is effectively the court dress of the upper nobility during the later eighteenth dynasty and throughout the nineteenth. In appearance it combines the short sleeved tunic or shirt with the elaborately pleated kilts and further recalls the earlier fashion of having a starched frontal 'apron' by being draped in such a way as to produce a long bag-like flap of material down the front of the garment (figure 21). The skirt is pleated over most of its area whilst on the tunic only the sleeves are so treated. The body of the tunic always appears, perhaps illusorily, to be of finer, more transparent fabric and it is possible that in some examples at least the sleeves were attached separately – there is indeed evidence for this practice from the

17

18

garments and textile remains which have survived. Furthermore the skirt is obviously draped and tucked over itself suggesting that it probably formed a garment separate from the tunic proper.

Examples survive on statues of New Kingdom scribes of the high-waisted midi-length nobles' skirt which was introduced in the Middle Kingdom (see figure 12). However such occurrences are so rare that these pieces are usually interpreted as reflecting an archaizing tendency on the part of the artist, especially as the figures also wear Middle Kingdom wigs and display other features more consistent with Middle than with New Kingdom art. Nevertheless these few examples serve as a useful way of introducing the next garment to be considered which not unreasonably may be assumed to have been influenced by, if not directly derived from, the Middle Kingdom high-waisted skirt. This is normally referred to as being the Vizier's (the chief Minister's) costume (figure 22) and in appearance is almost identical to the Middle Kingdom garment. It consists of an ankle length, high-waisted skirt the top edge of which passes either

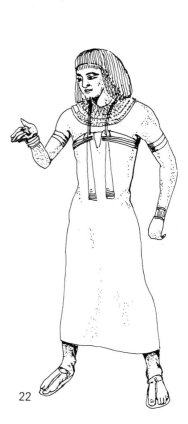

17 Official in a tunic, a kilt and an overskirt

18 A tunic and loincloth worn in combination

19 Thigh-length tunic with scalloped hem 'shaped' by use of a tied belt

20 All-over pleated kilt with sagging waistline typical of the later New Kingdom

21 See colour plate 5

22 The vizier's costume

directly below the breasts or tucks up into the armpits and is usually fringed. The bottom hem is normally shown curving down at the front in profile. It is supported by two very narrow straps attached to the top edge of the skirt fairly close together, about the width of the neck separating them, as a result of which they hug the inside of the neck as they pass over the shoulders. Apart from the shoulder straps the other main difference between this and the comparable Middle Kingdom garment is that it is not depicted as a wrap around skirt and so was presumably seamed and sewn up one edge. Nevertheless one example retains a skeuomorphic 'tab' as used to secure the Middle Kingdom skirts.

Again few examples of real officials' clothes have survived from the New Kingdom. Despite the large numbers of tombs which are known it should be borne in mind that many, indeed the majority of these were robbed of their contents in ancient times, usually within decades of the burial taking place. The pieces which are known are of coarser quality linen and are based on crude and simple designs which hardly mirror the elegant fashions of the tomb scenes. They comprise bag-like sleeveless shirts and tunics, lengths ranging from knee to ankle length (figure 23) and were made from a rectangle of linen sheeting. This was folded over and sewn up the sides. Slits were left at the top of the sides as armholes or for the attachment of separate sleeves; 'removable' sleeves seem to have been quite common in ancient Egypt. A keyhole-shaped neck opening was made, finished with a rolled hem and a pair of tie cords attached at the upper end of the narrower throat slot. Examples measure up to 122 cm or more long and about 76-89 cm wide. Occasionally if the end piece of a bolt of cloth was used in its manufacture the garment could have a warp fringe on one edge. Other, inadvertent decoration comes from natural variation of colour in the warp threads which can produce broad but irregular bands of lighter or darker threads giving a muted striped effect.

Flimsy linen shawls, about 76 x 89 cm have been found. The wardrobe of the architect Kha which was discovered packed into chests in his tomb at Deir el Medina included four shawls in addition to 17 sleeveless tunics, 26 shirts and about 50 triangular loincloths (figure 99).

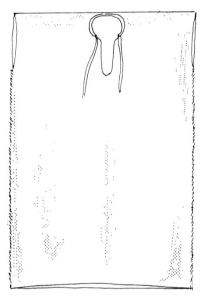

23 Bag-like tunic based on surviving examples from tombs

4 Women

Although perhaps not depicted quite as frequently as men, women played an important part in ancient Egyptian life and are commonly found in the tomb scenes both as the tomb owner's wife and daughters and as servant girls, dancers and musicians. A common form of statuary depicts husband and wife seated side by side. The wife usually sits to the husband's left with one arm around his shoulder in a gesture of affection and is often conventionally represented fractionally shorter to indicate a slightly subservient position. It is noticeable in Egyptian art, both statuary and tomb paintings, that men are usually painted with a reddish-brown skin whilst women have much paler yellowish skin. This is assumed to be a way of indicating that men, who spent their time working in the open fields, soon acquired a dark sun tan whereas women who spent most of their time indoors in the harem remained somewhat pale. Whilst this may have been true for royalty and the upper classes it was certainly not the case with the peasantry and women are often depicted working in the fields assisting with the harvest where they would soon have acquired all the rugged appearance of the menfolk.

Old Kingdom

The most frequently encountered women's garments are long, not quite ankle-length, linen dresses (figure 24). They are shown as being very tight fitting and in the finer examples hug the contours of the body impossibly closely. They end either just below or just above the breasts and were held up by two tapering shoulder straps widest at the point of attachment to the skirt and narrowest on top of the shoulders; these were often made of or decorated with beadwork. In the majority of instances the shoulder straps probably covered the breasts as is regularly the case on figurines. However the two dimensional tomb scenes normally show the breast exposed but this is purely a convention of Egyptian art which dictated that the torso be drawn in profile but the dress in front view so that the essential elements of both were clearly recognizable in the depiction. Dresses were frequently made from fabrics dyed in bright colours – green, blue, red and yellow – as well as being bleached white. Sometimes they were further adorned with beadwork patterns or had entire bead 'nets' overlaid on them.

The peasant women wore similar dresses but probably of coarser material and therefore looser fitting to the extent that on occasions a belt or

24   Woman's linen dress held up by two shoulder straps

tie was needed to prevent the dress interfering with one's tasks (figure 25).

Another accessory worn in conjunction with this type of dress was a thin waist-length wrap or shawl thrown lightly over the shoulders and pulled across the chest to cover the breasts (figure 26).

Considerably more modern in appearance is a long sleeveless dress obviously derived from the garment which we have just considered. However the shoulder straps are much wider, though still tapering, and are wide enough to fully cover the breasts effectively forming a low V-neck. Note that the sides of the dress fit much higher into the armpits as a result of widening the straps (figure 27).

An unusual instance of women wearing kilts is found in a fifth dynasty tomb scene depicting musicians, dancers and singers. The women singers wear the typical long dress with shoulder straps as already described. The dancers however wear a kilt which reaches not quite to their knees and seems to sit on the hips rather than on the waist (figure 28). It is supported by a linen belt with a simple tie and in some instances was pleated. It was so wrapped as to just meet down the front to facilitate movement such as kicking the legs up into the air. Their upper bodies are bare except for a thin sash or ribbon, also apparently of white linen, which encircles their bodies just above the waist and passes over the chest diagonally to form an X and goes around the back of the neck. They also wear a simple collar and what can only be described as a 'choker' around their neck.

In another scene dancing girls are dressed in a briefer, loincloth type of apron similar to that worn by labourers and fishermen except that it has a piece pendent from the back of the waist (figure 29). Their professional headgear comprises a red ball or disc attached to a ribbon hanging from the top of their heads.

No actual examples either of women's kilts or of the ubiquitous dress with shoulder straps have been discovered. However, nine dresses in two grades of linen were found in the tomb of a lady at Deshasheh very similar to the man's tunic described above. A high waisted skirt reaching from immediately below the breasts to the feet was made from a single piece of linen folded over and sewn down one edge, usually the left (figure 30). Some have weft fringes down the seamed edge. As in the case of the comparable man's garment two pieces of linen were sewn onto this forming the front yoke and sleeves and the identical back yoke and sleeves. The V-shaped neckline was pulled closed by three pairs of twisted flax strings at both front and back. The long sleeves were very narrow having been sewn up along the inside seam so as to leave a loose flap of material hanging down. It is possible that this practice was originally intended to leave a certain amount of surplus cloth for letting the sleeve out but that it subsequently became accepted as part of the fashion. The bottom hem and those on the wrists were rolled. All of these garments proved to be excessively long ranging between 140 cm and 172 cm and it has been estimated that they could not have been worn by anyone less than one and a half metres tall. In width they vary from 40 to 58 cm. Thus it seems probable that they were intended purely as part of the funerary

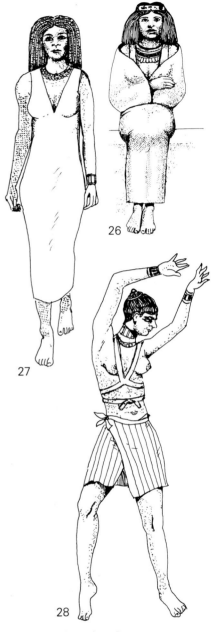

25   See colour plate 2

26   Long dress worn in conjunction with a waist length shawl

27   Long sleeveless V-necked dress

28   A dancer's kilt

22

equipment and were never destined to be worn in life and so not made to exact sizes. It is unlikely that they were to be worn pulled up and hanging over a girdle if only on the grounds of their remarkable resemblance to the modern Egyptian *galabiyeh*.

The excessive length could on the other hand be explained by examples of similar sleeved dresses found on other sites which preserve traces of horizontal pleating. Had the Deshasheh dresses been so treated it would have reduced their length considerably. The effect of the pleats would have been to make the garments warmer during cold evenings. However, the difficulty of preventing them dropping out meant that they had only a limited period of popularity. Although at least one example was found in a man's tomb the majority of such dresses are associated with women.

29 Dancer's loincloth with a ribbon hanging down the back

Middle Kingdom

Unlike modern times women's fashions were much more conservative than men's in ancient Egypt and they underwent relatively little change. It is not surprising therefore that the normal female garment for the upper and middle classes remained the fairly close fitting dress with two shoulder straps which has been described above. The Middle Kingdom dresses display a bright array of colours. As well as the plain bleached white linen very fine, almost transparent dresses are found together with self coloured examples; green seems to have been most popular. An assortment of designs and patterns is also found portrayed on the fabrics, many of them probably of applied beadwork. There is a variety of simple geometric designs (figure 31) such as rows of zig-zags; the four-petalled rosette is very common sometimes combined with a net or diamond pattern. Another frequently encountered design is what may be called the scale pattern consisting of coloured scales or scales and dots.

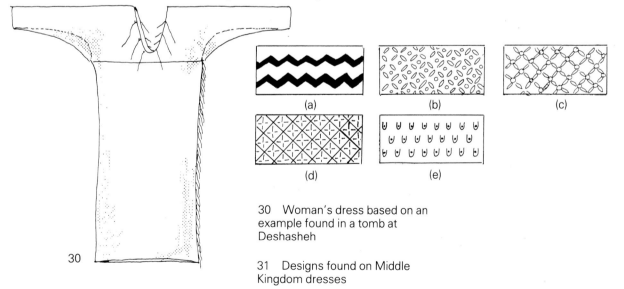

30

(a)   (b)   (c)

(d)   (e)

30 Woman's dress based on an example found in a tomb at Deshasheh

31 Designs found on Middle Kingdom dresses

The woollen blanket-like garment which we have seen was introduced in the Middle Kingdom for men was also worn by women. As with men it could be worn either over both shoulders or only one, usually the left. The former was most common for women however (figure 32). Women's versions often have a short fringe on the upper edge but lack the horizontal stripes so characteristic of men's.

As in the Old Kingdom women are rarely shown in kilts but again dancers are the exception and occur in knee-length kilts or skirts with vertical pleats. Elsewhere dancing, or rather skipping, women are seen in a longer, calf-length split skirt (figure 33) which does not seem to overlap as much as the kilts. It is tied at the front. In addition the women wear what is most likely to be the same as the short scarf or stole which we have already seen on noblemen. However the scene in question is badly preserved and it could be that we are dealing with straps actually attached to the waistband of the skirt though it is difficult to see what particular merit these would have had and the former interpretation seems most likely. They have the long festive dancers' ribbons trailing from the backs of their heads.

A less frequently depicted item but one which was probably much more common than the evidence suggests, especially amongst the lower classes, is the cane or straw kilt (figure 34). This has the appearance of being a rather stiff and cumbersome garment. The wearers' occupations, in this instance leading cattle, suggest the lower classes and this is perhaps reflected in their sagging pendulous breasts compared to the firm rounded breasts of the nobler women.

No real ladies' garments survive from this period though fragments of pleated linen were found in one queen's tomb.

New Kingdom

The comments made above in the section dealing with New Kingdom men's garments apply equally here and the New Kingdom women's fashions witness a change over earlier styles. What are best described as more 'modern looking' garments are introduced in the eighteenth dynasty and, as with men, following the artistic freedom of the Amarna period, the late eighteenth and nineteenth dynasty vogue was for an abundance of pleats on voluminous and lavishly draped garments. Despite this, however, women's costume tended to remain rather more conservative than men's and we see less change and fewer developments of individual styles than with men's clothing.

Having said that it is necessary to begin the section dealing with women's costume of the New Kingdom by stating that the familiar long sheath dress supported by shoulder straps as worn throughout the Old and Middle Kingdoms is found not infrequently in New Kingdom scenes. Although most often seen on ranking personal maid servants it obviously retained a wider usage than might be supposed from the evidence.

The wives and ladies of the nobility in the earlier New Kingdom wore a long ankle-length sleeveless dress probably consisting of little other than

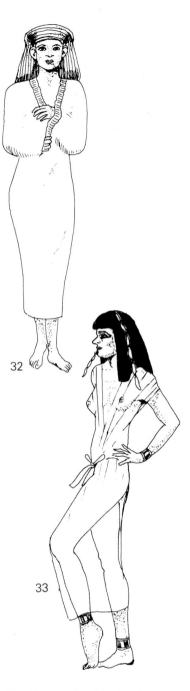

32 The woollen blanket like garment normally worn over both shoulders by women

33 Dancing woman in a long split skirt

34 See colour plate 4

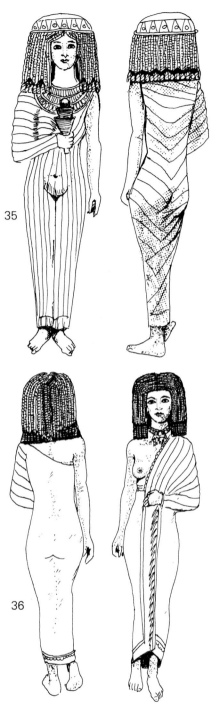

a piece of linen folded over and sewn up two edges with gaps left for the arms and neck. Certainly this is more consistent with the remains of actual textiles which have survived in the tombs though the wall paintings depict brilliantly white bleached fine linen clothes which hug the contours of the body and generally display a simple elegance which belies the bald description and the surviving tatters. Such tight fitting sleeveless dresses are occasionally, but not commonly in the New Kingdom, found worn over one shoulder only, usually the left leaving the right shoulder bare. Sometimes the right breast is covered by the garment and at other times left exposed.

Closely related in appearance to the simple dresses described above is a robe consisting of a single piece of material which is draped and wrapped around the body rather like a sari. The material of these robes was often pleated and the borders were usually fringed, often more elaborately decorated. The two examples illustrated here are typical and the two methods of draping mirror the style of the simple dresses. In one (figure 35) the drape covers both shoulders whilst in the other (figure 36) it passes over only one shoulder leaving the other shoulder, arm and breast almost down to the waist exposed. In examples where dresses and robes pass over one shoulder only it is usually the left one thereby leaving the right arm with greater freedom of movement an observation which suggests that the ancient Egyptians were, like us, predominantly right-handed. Figures wearing robes of these types are normally shown with one arm held across the front of their waist as if holding the garment together though in practice it would doubtless have been pinned with one of the many decorative bronze, bone or wooden dress pins known from excavations or held by ties attached to the edges of the cloth.

The queens of the period wore similar garments but of finer, softer material. In addition Tutankhamun's queen is seen wearing a long vertically pleated wrap-round skirt trailing on the floor at the back and held at the waist by a tied belt the two ends of which are almost as long as the skirt itself (figure 37). On her upper body she wears a pleated cape knotted at the front so as to cover her breasts but not her waist. This example is quite long at the back though shorter versions are known which reach only to the hips. The skirt and cape are of diaphanous linen bleached to a brilliant white whilst the cloth belt was in a self colour such as pale orange-red.

As is to be expected the women of the lower orders had less fine clothes than those we have been considering above. After the wives of nobles and the queens the women most commonly depicted in the tomb scenes are entertainers, that is musicians and dancers, and servant girls either serving at banquets or attending to the toilet of a noble lady.

Although the women of these categories are depicted in the long sheath dress more commonly they are effectively naked and wear only a narrow decorated belt around their hips, of dubious if any function. Indeed it was probably purely ornamental as there is no suggestion that anything attached to it and passed between the legs to cover the pubic region (figure 38).

35   Sari-like garment draped over both shoulders

36   The same garment worn over only one shoulder

37   See colour plate 6

Less usual garments for servants are the sleeved dresses illustrated in figure 39. These are tight fitting ankle length garments with elbow length sleeves and a straight high neckline at the back. The front of the neck has a keyhole shaped opening fastened by ties. Another scene depicting a young woman pulling flax shows her in a similar dress but with long sleeves reaching to the wrists.

A very acrobatic dancer drawn tumbling over backwards onto her hands in an unusual depiction wears a short skirt or kilt. It falls longer over the buttocks but is pulled up at the front presumably to allow her more freedom of movement for her energetic pursuits. Apart from this skirt and large annular earrings she is naked with neither a blouse nor sandals (figure 40). The skirt is coloured black with decoration in white and red though in view of the nature of the piece this probably merely indicates that the fabric was decorated rather than being an accurate portrayal of the decoration itself. The drawing is an ancient artist's sketch done on a flake of waste limestone discarded from the excavation of a tomb. Such sketches and doodles often break away from the stereotypes and conventions of Egyptian art as rendered in tomb scenes which, as mentioned in the introduction, are meant to portray an ideal world suitable for eternity. As such it may perhaps represent more what the dancing girls of the period wore than do the tomb paintings themselves.

It must be remembered that the servant girls and probably also many of the dancers and musicians would have been permanently employed on one of the noble estates or by the larger households of officials. Thus some of their clothes at least would have been provided rather like a uniform or set of overalls in many jobs today or else they would have formed a part of their remuneration all of which would have been paid in kind. Whether the servants who wear dresses are more senior to or have some other distinction of status over those who wear only the thin girdles cannot be decided without further research though it would seem unlikely. More plausible is that the alternation between dresses and girdles seen in the tomb paintings is a device of the artist to allow some variations in the composition of the scene.

38   Serving girl in typically scant attire

39   See colour plate 6

40   See colour plate 6

42b

42a

Groups of mourning women are depicted in the private tombs of the New Kingdom so frequently that it has been asserted that there may have been professional troupes of them who attended at the funerals of those who could afford them. They normally wore plainer versions of the noble ladies' clothes, either the plain dress in the earlier New Kingdom or pleated robes from the late eighteenth dynasty onwards. When shown in isolation mourning women and widows are bare breasted as this was a mark of grief though occasionally members of a professional group are shown with their breasts covered. They formed part of the funeral procession weeping and waving their arms rhythmically or else beating their head and/or breast with alternate hands. Another sign of grief was to throw dust on oneself and the women would probably have indulged in the present day Arab practice of ululating, a high pitched warbling made by rapidly moving the tongue, between their bouts of wailing and weeping in a more conventional manner.

Peasant women are not often depicted in the New Kingdom scenes but would doubtless have worn fairly simple clothes though not necessarily coarse or in any way crude as there is evidence of a considerable cottage industry in textiles. Most women working out in the fields would have worn a simple skirt such as that illustrated here (figure 41) with nothing on their torso. The ancient Egyptians do not seem to have found exposure of the female breast in any way immodest. The example here is fairly long at below knee length and was probably seamed rather than being wrap-round.

Another scene shows a peasant woman with her child who is supported by a 'sling' formed from a piece of white linen which is wrapped around both mother and child. The exact nature of the garment is unclear due to the poor draughtsmanship of the ancient artist and the woman appears to be otherwise naked (figure 42a). It may well be that she has in fact removed her own dress in order to use it to support her child in this way. In a later relief a woman in a short, knee-length dress or skirt supports her child by means of a similar sling but made from a single broad piece of cloth (figure 42b).

41   See colour plate 7

42a   A woman nursing her child

42b   Woman supporting her child
by means of a cloth sling

5 The King

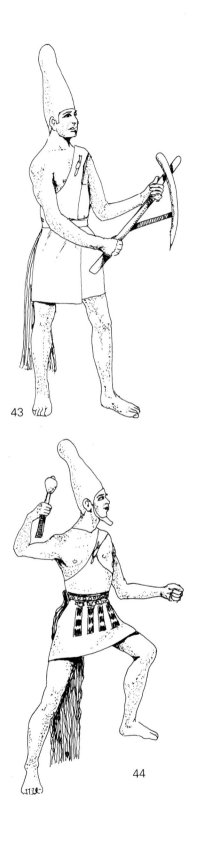

One of the earliest detailed depictions of an Egyptian king occurs on a decorated limestone macehead of King Scorpion from the very end of the predynastic period. This depicts, amongst other scenes, a king recognizable as such by his head-dress which is the characteristic White Crown of Upper Egypt (below p. 35). He holds a hoe in both hands with which he is opening up an irrigation ditch thereby symbolizing the prosperity to come during his reign. His garment is a mid-thigh length wrap round tunic which is fastened only over his left shoulder leaving his right one bare. Another mark of royalty is the bull's tail which hangs from the back of his waist (figure 43).

Another early detailed depiction of pharaoh occurs on the palette of Narmer (figure 44), probably the king who united Upper Egypt and Lower Egypt into a single political state and the last king of the predynastic period. He is likewise shown in a short tunic fastened over the left shoulder with a dress pin. He wears a decorated belt with geometric patterns and an elaborate panel adorns the front of the skirt. The design is reminiscent of tied bundles of reeds as used in the architecture of this remote period. There is a cow's head with sharply incurving horns on top of each bundle. Again a bull's tail from the rear of the waistband is a mark of royalty. Narmer is shown in the White Crown on one side of his palette and in the Red Crown of Lower Egypt on the other hence the tendency by scholars to attribute to him the unification of Egypt. Although depicted barefoot he is on both sides of the palette followed by an attendant carrying a pair of sandals. The attendant is dressed in a triangular loincloth.

This type of tunic seems to have remained current throughout the Early Dynastic period and king Sekhemkhet is seen still wearing it in the third dynasty. One slight modification is to the rectangular panel at the front which hangs slightly lower than the hem of the tunic itself.

Old Kingdom

The kings of the fourth, fifth and sixth dynasties seem to have preferred a short kilt, at least for ceremonial or official use. This kilt, in ancient Egyptian called a *shendyt*, reached only to the middle of the thighs and was cut or otherwise tailored so that when worn it gave a tripartite effect in front view. The two side pieces of the kilt curved gently from the centre of the waistband to the outer edges of the thighs and a tapering flap of material hung down the front but behind the two side pieces (figure 45). It was held

43

44

28

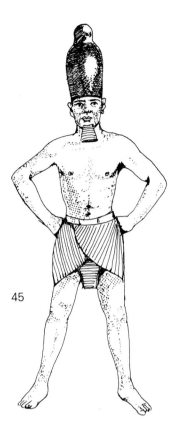

up by means of a belt. Plain examples of such kilts are found but ones with radiating pleats on the skirt and horizontal pleats on the descending flap are much more common.

The kings also wore the standard nobles' kilts with tailored curved overlap or starched triangular frontal apron. As befitted his rank however these royal kilts were most elaborately pleated or decorated.

Another royal garment from the earliest period but surviving into the Old Kingdom has been called a 'festival robe'. It is seen to best advantage on a statue of the second dynasty king Khasekhem (figure 46). This mid-calf length garment, rather like a modern dressing gown, overlaps at the front and is tailored so as to produce a V-neck effect. There is no collar and it sits low on the back of the neck but appears slightly thickened on the upper edge suggesting a rolled hem.

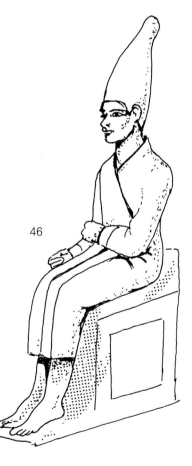

43   King Scorpion as depicted on his decorated macehead

44   King Narmer as he appears on his decorated slate palette

45   The *shendyt*-kilt often worn by the king

46   The royal 'festival robe'

Middle Kingdom

During the Middle Kingdom the dress of the king changes very little from earlier periods. The pleated *shendyt*-kilt remains popular as does the knee-length kilt with starched apron at the front. The example illustrated here (figure 47) has a thin vertical panel of decoration down the front ending in two royal uraeus serpents. This adjunct is obviously derived from the decorative panel which we noticed on Narmer's tunic. The king also wears a *nemes*-head-dress (described on page 36) and a pin and knot amulet suspended from a thread around his neck.

The earliest royal dress encountered on the Scorpion mace head and the palette of Narmer was still worn in the form of a short tunic with a single strap over one (the right) shoulder either pinned or knotted for support. In most examples the king also wears a belt, the familiar bull's tail and the double crown of united Egypt.

One of the most important of the Egyptian royal festivals was the *heb-sed* festival or royal jubilee which was usually celebrated after thirty years of reign though some later kings held them more regularly. The ceremony is believed to be a survival from a prehistoric time when the king was thought to have exhausted his powers after thirty years. In order to ensure continuing prosperity and fertility therefore the old king was ritually slaughtered and a new young king was installed. In historic times the king merely underwent an enacted sacrifice and after running a ritual race-course and performing various other ceremonies was deemed rejuvenated and he embarked on a further thirty years reign. Obviously special garments were worn for this ceremony and the one illustrated here consists of a short tunic worn over both shoulders. In this particular example the king is wearing the Red crown of Lower Egypt (figure 48).

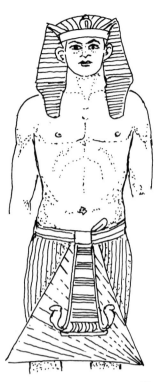

47

48

47   Royal kilt with decorated panel down the front

48   A king dressed for the Jubilee Festival

New Kingdom

Throughout the New Kingdom kings are still to be found dressed in the archaic tunic with single shoulder strap as already described. This garment retains the royal attribute of a long animal's tail, probably bull's or giraffe's, with a belt and rectangular front panel which descends just below the hem of the tunic. Pharaohs are particularly portrayed in this costume in scenes of a ritual nature where they are being presented to or led by a god.

In her mortuary temple at Deir el-Bahri Queen Hatshepsut, who for the most part had herself depicted in the monuments as if she were male and generally used the masculine pronoun in her inscriptions, is shown wearing the typical Egyptian woman's sheath dress with two tapering shoulder straps (figure 49). However it is immediately discernible as being royal as it combines all the features of the archaic tunic; animal's tail, belt and long scarf-like panel down the front in this instance with striped decoration and fringed. Furthermore the dress is cut short just above the knees reflecting the length of the archaic royal tunics; sheath dresses proper are always ankle length.

Likewise the Old Kingdom *shendyt*-kilt continues to be worn, both plain and pleated, as well as the knee length kilt with a starched apron at the front. The latter are usually worn with a long sporran-like flap down the front embellished with symbols of royalty, especially uraeus serpents. On occasions the two styles of kilt are shown combined as if the *shendyt*-kilt were being worn over a conventional kilt with starched apron (figure 50).

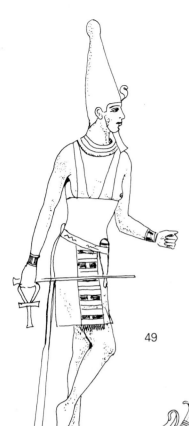

49

50

49   Queen Hatshepsut in a typical sheath dress with additions drawn from the archaic royal tunic

50   Two types of kilt worn combined

31

In at least one instance the kilt with starched front is worn with a long, ankle-length, diaphanous under skirt below. A diagonal sash across the torso passes over the right shoulder (figure 51).

From the Amarna period onwards royal dress reflects the changed styles seen in the noble's and women's costume of the period. Thus the king is often seen in an all-over pleated kilt with the sagging concave waistline introduced by Amenophis IV and continuing into the nineteenth dynasty. The illustration here is based on a small figurine found in Tutankhamun's tomb and is a typical kilt of the type (figure 52). The hem hangs lower at the back but is pulled up over the thighs into the waist band at the front. A long decorated flap hangs down the front with streamers or ties at either side. In this example the belt is thicker at the back than at the front and is very ornate. In the nineteenth dynasty this type of kilt is often worn in conjunction with a short sleeved shirt or tunic (figure 53).

The kilt was obviously very much a ceremonial garment, especially as it is portrayed on the monuments, and in private moments the king would doubtless have worn garments similar to the simple long tunics discussed above. An unusual statue of Amenophis III depicts him not as a virile, strong, young king but as the fat old man which he was in later life. On this he wears a long tunic the bottom hem of which is fringed and reaches to the instep (figure 54). It has been suggested that this may reflect an Asiatic fashion and although the upper part of the tunic is obscured the lower part is not inconsistent with the clothes worn by Syro-Palestinian tribute bearers. Certainly there was considerable traffic and exchange of goods between Egypt and Syria-Palestine during the eighteenth and nineteenth dynasties either in the form of diplomatic exchanges of gifts between kings, payment of tribute by vassal kinglets, plundering of booty by victorious armies or, despite the meagre evidence for it, commercial trading itself. It would not be at all remarkable therefore to find a foreign garment being worn by an Egyptian at this height of empire. Above the tunic Amenophis is wearing a thin vertically pleated overgarment worn over the shoulders and pulled across the chest where it is secured by a tie and loop; it is left to fall open over the lower part of the tunic. It has very much the appearance of a modern chiffon negligée and, even for Egyptian fashions, has a very feminine appearance.

51 Starched kilt with long underskirt and a chest sash

PLATE 1 *A weaver's workshop based on a wooden model of Middle Kingdom date*

PLATE 2 *Centre: 25 A looser fitting working woman's dress with belt*

Right: 87 Workman in a shortened kilt

Left: 89 A hunter's tunic

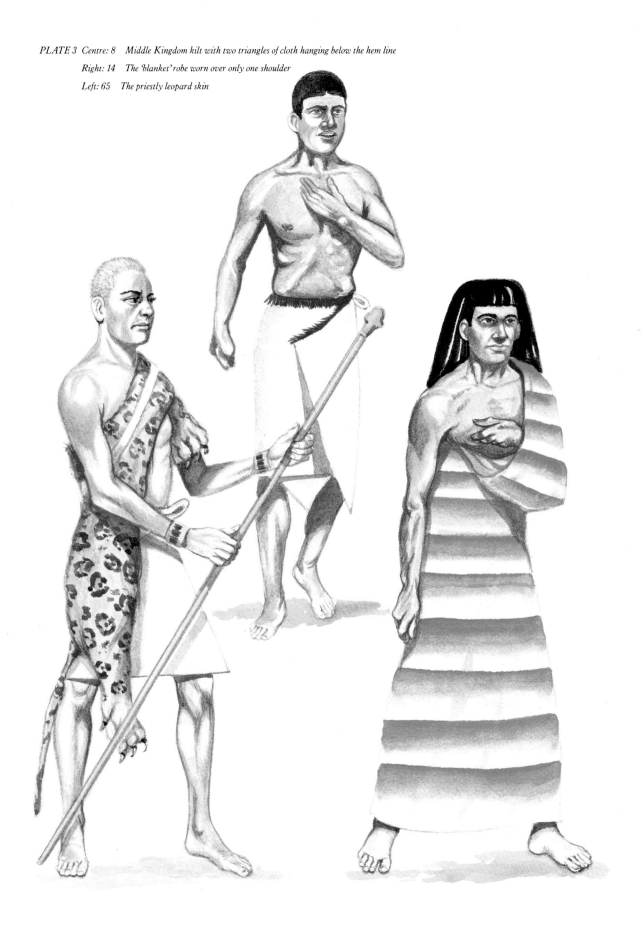

PLATE 3 Centre: 8   Middle Kingdom kilt with two triangles of cloth hanging below the hem line

Right: 14   The 'blanket' robe worn over only one shoulder

Left: 65   The priestly leopard skin

PLATE 4 Right: 34   Kilt made from cane or straw

Centre: 114   Beja herdsman in a simple loincloth

Left: Typical Middle Kingdom woman's dress

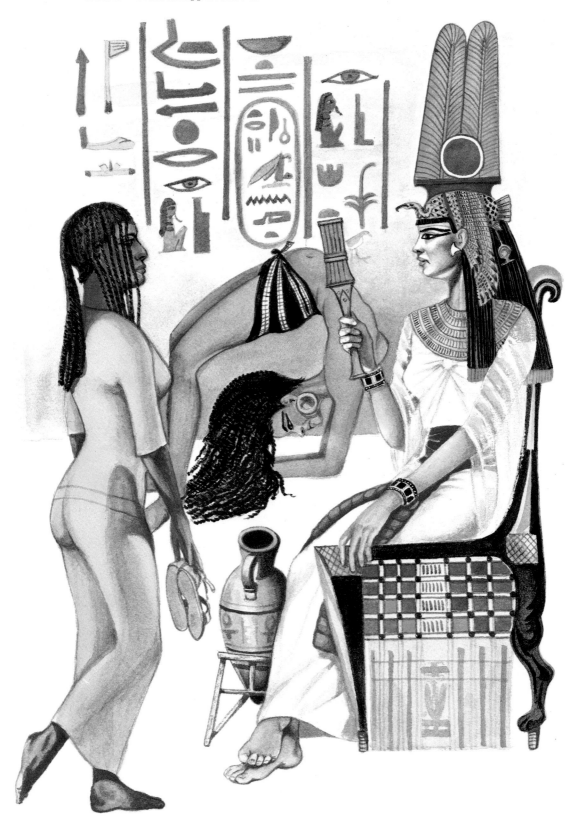

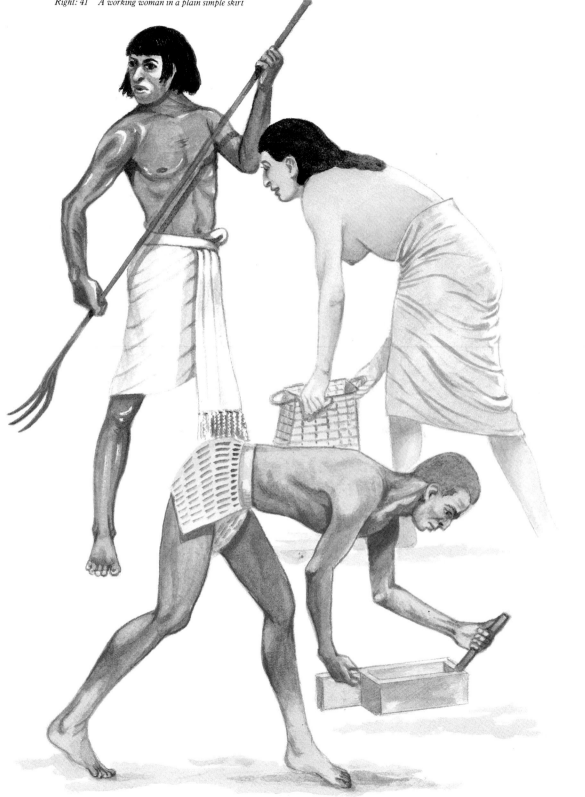

PLATE 8 *Left: 103   A scale armour shirt Centre: 107   A Philistine soldier Right: Egyptian archer*

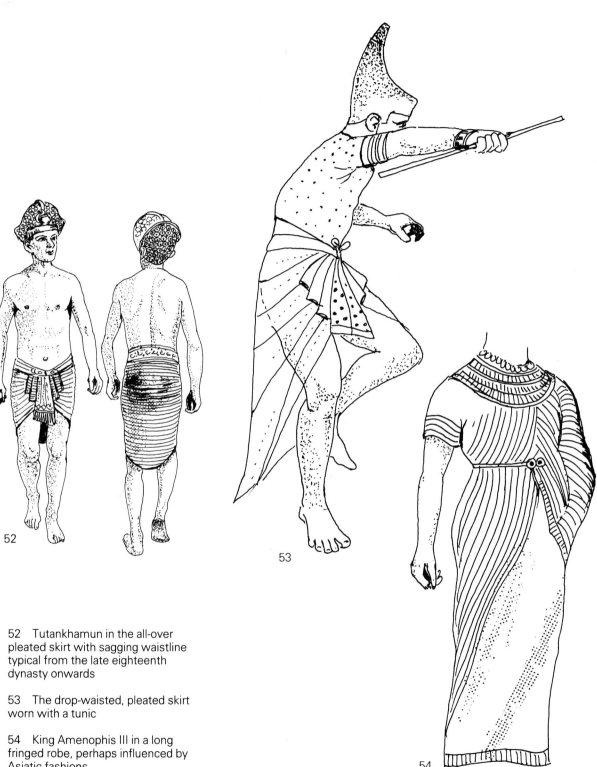

52   Tutankhamun in the all-over
pleated skirt with sagging waistline
typical from the late eighteenth
dynasty onwards

53   The drop-waisted, pleated skirt
worn with a tunic

54   King Amenophis III in a long
fringed robe, perhaps influenced by
Asiatic fashions

The king also wore what we have above described as the court dress for the nobility namely the all-over pleated kilt with a long bag-like piece at the front together with a tunic with short pleated sleeves. Not dissimilar, though fussier in overall effect, is a costume consisting of a calf-length kilt or skirt supported by a decorated belt and two long ties with single tassels at the ends (figure 55). The royal 'sporran' with its fringe of uraeus serpents at the bottom and the animal's tail down the back, probably here an imitation one, should also be noted. Over the kilt the king wears a long diaphanous 'cape' which extends to his ankles. This is thrown over both shoulders and the ends are knotted together in the centre of his chest. As well as having fine vertical pleats the outer cape is fringed along the bottom edge and up one side and is decorated all round with a narrow border of alternating red and green dots.

Amongst the hoard of funerary equipment recovered from the tomb of king Tutankhamun were many items of clothing. These are usually over-shadowed in the publications by the 'treasures' from the tomb yet in fact form a very important addition to the stock of real garments from ancient Egypt. Included in his wardrobe were about one hundred loincloths sometimes paired up with kilts, several shirts or short tunics, tens of children's garments, thirty gloves, a priestly leopard skin and two cloth imitation leopard skins with gilded wooden heads and gold claws.

The most outstanding garment however was Carter's number 367j found in a box in the tomb's storeroom (figure 56). This is a tunic made from plain but fine quality linen with a fringe along the bottom edge and decorated with bands of pattern weave and embroidery. Its manufacture probably followed the normal pattern of folding a single piece of linen and sewing it

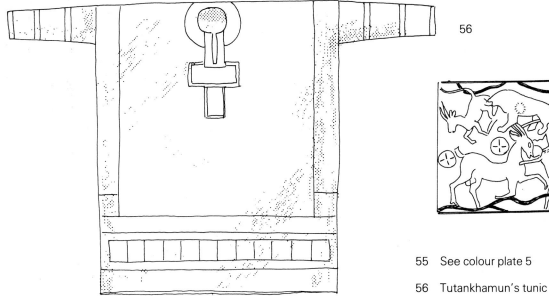

56

55 See colour plate 5

56 Tutankhamun's tunic

34

together along the selvedges leaving slits into which the sleeves were subsequently sewn. An opening with a keyhole slot was cut in the front, below the line of the fold, for the head and neck; cutting it in this position allowed the neck line at the back to remain fairly high. The sleeves were made from even finer linen and it is possible that they fell from the elbow to the wrist as the tunic tends to drape itself over the upper arms. The piece is approximately 114 cm long by 96 cm wide with 36 cm sleeves. Several similar but sleeveless and undecorated tunics were also found in the tomb ranging from knee length to examples which must have trailed on the floor. The width of tunic was such that it must surely have been worn in conjunction with a belt or cloth girdle to give it more shape. Several items were found in the tomb which could have fulfilled this purpose.

The exceptional feature of Tutankhamun's tunic however is the well preserved decorative bands and the unique chest panel in the shape of a cross. The neck opening is outlined with a band in which the main decorative element is cartouches containing one of Tutankhamun's royal names, Neb-Khepru-Re. The bottom borders are embroidered, a rare form of decoration on extant Egyptian textiles. Only two embroidery stitches are known to have been used for certain – outline stitch and chain stitch. The embroidery was done in separate small panels which were sewn together before application to the tunic. The motifs include palmettes, sphinxes, gryphons and hunting scenes very reminiscent of designs on Syrian ivories. Some of the textiles in the tomb were decorated in warp weave, others with tapestry weave. Such woven decoration was usually applied in bands down the sides, both at the front and back, round the bottom of the skirt and round the neck opening. Many garments had the more usual decoration of applied beadwork or gold and faience sequins. The 'sequins' were normally circular or rosette shaped pieces of gold, silver or blue faience 1 to 4 cm in diameter and either pierced with holes or made with a lug for sewing them onto the cloth. One tunic was decorated with three thousand gold rosettes.

Comparatively few other royal clothes have been recovered. Scraps of material decorated in tapestry weave were found in the tomb of Tuthmosis IV and a girdle of Rameses III is known. The woven bands have simple geometric arrangements of squares, diamonds, chevrons and zigzags.

Crowns and royal head-dresses

The two basic crowns of ancient Egypt were the White Crown of Upper Egypt and the Red Crown of Lower Egypt. The White Crown (see figures 44 and 45) is always painted white and consisted of a tall ovoid head-dress, possibly of starched linen, waisted near the top and then expanded into a sphere. Put more graphically it could be described as a rugby ball, truncated at one end and with a tennis ball stuck on the other. The crown of Lower Egypt was, as its name implies, red and it is possible that, originally at least, it was made from reeds or some form of basketwork (figure 57). It comprised a flat topped hat extending down the back of the

57   The Red Crown of Lower Egypt

neck. A taller section projected upwards at the rear from the base of which a single length of reed curved out and up into a spiral. On most occasions pharaoh is shown wearing the Double Crown, simply a combination of the White and Red in which the White Upper Egyptian crown rested on the flat top of the Red one; the spiralling reed was either omitted or sprouted from about two thirds of the way up the White Crown (figure 58).

The height of the Double Crown, if not the weight, would have rendered it very clumsy and it would doubtless have been worn in reality only on very special occasions. It is much more common for the kings of the Old Kingdom and later to be shown wearing a head-dress (Egyptian *nemes*) which is essentially a wig-cover. Some were certainly made of linen, starched or stiffened in some way, whilst others may have been made of leather or other more rigid materials. The front of the *nemes* is normally surmounted by a uraeus, a device in the form of a female cobra rearing in rage with its wide expanded throat and coiling body.

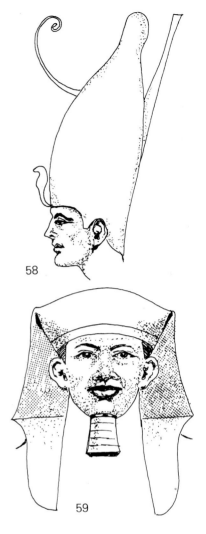

58

Plain *nemes* headcloths, obviously made of linen, and with neither decoration nor the uraeus can be found (figure 59). Occasionally the lappets which hang over the front of the shoulders are shown with horizontal pleats or stripes whilst the rest of the *nemes* is plain. Most frequently however the *nemes* has stripes all over, sometimes a double stripe, sometimes a triple. Only rarely does the hair or wig protrude from beneath the headband of the *nemes*. The most famous example of this head-dress is the one depicted on Tutankhamun's gold mask.

After the state crowns and the *nemes* the next most frequent headgear seen on pharaohs is the Blue Crown, Egyptian *khepresh*, so called because it is usually coloured blue (figure 60). It occurs for the first time on royal monuments at the end of the seventeenth dynasty and is often wrongly referred to as being the 'War Crown'. In fact the monuments show that it was worn on many varied occasions – ceremonial, military and private. In the most detailed portrayals the crown is shown covered all over with small circular studs, a uraeus serpent rearing up at the front and two long streamers trailing pendent from the back.

59

Many other crowns and head-dresses can be found in the reliefs and paintings. Most of these are of a religious nature being specifically connected with certain gods and their worship or their role in the ceremonies and festivals. Some of these will be considered below in chapter six. A famous relief of much later date in the Graeco-Roman temple at Dendereh portrays twenty three different crowns.

58 The Double Crown

59   A *nemes*-headcloth

60 The Blue Crown

60

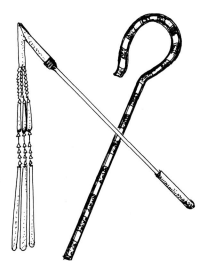

61

Other regalia

The two universal symbols of Egyptian sovereignty were the crook and the flail and were held by the king, one in each hand, on all important occasions as well as being the characteristic attributes of mummiform representations of the god Osiris in his capacity as king of the underworld with whom the dead king becomes one. Actual specimens of the shepherd's crook (Egyptian *hekat*) range in length from 35 to 90 cm and are usually made of wood and covered with sheet gold. In paintings they are normally coloured yellow with blue or black bands probably representing bronze rings used to secure the gold (figure 61).

The flail (Egyptian *nekhakha*) appears from the first dynasty onwards and as well as being a symbol of royalty especially associated with the *heb-sed* or jubilee festival it is also found held by some of the gods and incorporated into various cult objects. It consists of a wooden rod with an acute angle at one end from which hang three pendent pieces. In the examples which have survived these consist variously of simple straps, cords, rolls of linen or strings of conical, cylindrical and drop-shaped beads (figure 61). Such an instrument obviously could not be used as a whip and one theory, based on its close association with the shepherd's crook and with more recent Mediterranean parallels, interprets it as being an instrument for gathering ladanum resin.

Other items which were on occasion carried by pharaoh include the *'ankh* symbol of life and the *was*-sceptre (figure 62) a straight staff forked at one end and carved with the head of the sacred animal of the god Seth at the other. Pear shaped stone mace-heads on a wooden shaft are often wielded by the king in conventionalized scenes showing him smiting the enemies of Egypt whom he grasps by the hair with his free hand.

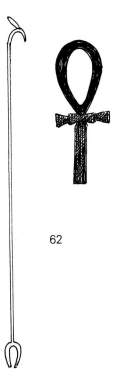

62

61   The royal 'crook' and 'flail', the symbols of kingship

62   (a) The *was*-sceptre
     (b) the 'ankh symbol of life

6 Priests and gods

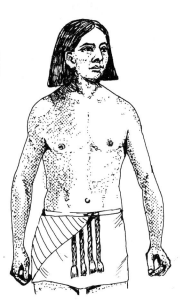

PRIESTS

The popular image of ancient Egypt is one of mummies, tombs, mysterious gods and a general pre-occupation with death. This is not a fair picture however as the Egyptians were very fond of life and references to singing, dancing, sports, drunkenness, love poems and such like suggest that they were just as fond of having a good time as anyone else. In fact it is rather the case that they clung to life so tenaciously that they could not bear the thought of death being the end of things and so conceived the very elaborate afterlife in which they believed so vividly that the whole funerary system evolved around it. The afterlife itself was visualized simply as a bigger, better, more idealized version of earthly existence. Nevertheless an overall impression of morbid obsession with death lingers on in the popular mind largely because the evidence which has come down to us from ancient Egypt concerns the funerary cult; that is it consists of objects and texts intended for funerary use deposited and depicted in the tombs. These have survived in remarkably large numbers, many virtually intact, due to their location in the barren desert and cliffs flanking the Nile, areas which are useless for any other purpose. The ancient towns and villages however have long since disappeared through re-building and pressure for more intensive use of the narrow strip of valuable agricultural land to either side of the river.

Two basic functions of the priesthood can be distinguished. Firstly there were cult priests, those who served the cult of a particular god, and mortuary priests, those who tended the funerary needs of the dead by providing regular offerings and ensuring that their tomb remained intact. It was quite common however for cult priests to act as mortuary priests for various individuals as well as serving the god. Several classes of priests can be distinguished the lowliest being the *wab*-priest followed by 'god's fathers' and 'prophets'. These formed the basic staff of the temples. In addition there were various specialist priests such as the lector priest, a high ranking priest responsible for the temple records and sacred books. The priesthood was not a vocation in ancient Egypt and it is not unusual to encounter civil servants or soldiers for example being promoted into the priesthood or vice versa. Their livelihood was based on consumption of the offerings made to the gods or the funerary chapels. A meal was presented to the cult image of a god or to the offering niche in a tomb chapel and the god or the deceased respectively magically partook of the food. After a

63

63 Priest in a typical Old Kingdom kilt but with tasselled cords hanging down the front

64

64 Priest wearing a distinctive collar associated with the high priest of Memphis

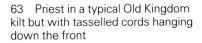

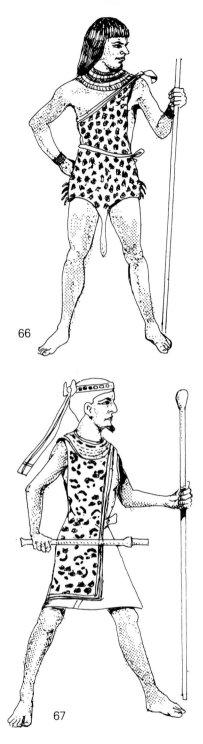

66

67

sufficiently decent interval the food was removed and eaten by the priests. In addition temples had large, generally self-sufficient estates attached to them and similar provision but obviously on a much smaller scale was made for the tombs of the higher and richer nobility.

For the most part priests dressed in the fashion of the nobility but were expected to wear only garments made of fine linen. They had to have clean shaven heads and chins. Only the specialist priests had distinguishing garments as described below though it is possible that on occasions priests dressed in costumes and perhaps even masks associated with certain gods whose presence was needed in a particular ceremony. However no such masks have been found.

Old and Middle Kingdoms

One Old Kingdom figure of a funerary priest shows him wearing the typical nobles' kilt with pleated curved overlap but down the front hang four twisted threads with tassels on the ends (figure 63). Whether these are specifically associated with his priestly role or are simply an individualistic decorative addition is difficult to judge due to the paucity of other such examples. However at least one other depiction has a kilt with tassels, in this instance five, projecting below the bottom hem. This figure wears the Memphite priestly collar described below and is therefore obviously a priest.

Another Old Kingdom official, called Khai-Bau-Sokar, held several priestly titles. He is also depicted in the short nobles kilt with curved pleated overlap; the pleated part of the kilt is yellow, the remainder white. Two wedge-shaped tabs, not to be confused with the tasselled cords discussed above, hang down from the inside of the kilt at centre front (figure 64). Connected with his priestly office is the distinctive necklace or collar which is associated with the high priest of Memphis. This takes the form of a jackal or jackal-like animal whose body is extremely elongated and forms a U-shape; its front paws are bent at the knees and raised in a position of prayer or adoration.

One of the most distinctive specialist priestly garments consists of a cured leopard skin draped over the body. It was usually worn in conjunction with a short knee-length kilt of either the plain or starched apron variety (figure 65). It was normally worn so that the tail hung down the back of the legs and the front paws came round the shoulders onto the upper arms. The paws are often shown complete with claws. The animal's head was left on the skin and this was thrown over one shoulder. When priests clad in such garments are depicted walking they often pull the rear of the skin round to the front and hold the tail up horizontally in one hand.

Other depictions suggest that sometimes the skins were 'tailored' to provide a better fitting garment. This could include partial tailoring such as figure 66 in which the tail and hind legs have been left on the skin unaltered whilst the forepart has been cut to form a diagonal across the chest resembling the early royal tunics. It is tied or pinned over the left shoulder and held in at the waist by a belt or knotted cord.

65   See colour plate 3

66   A partially tailored leopard skin

67   A rectangular, possibly imitation, leopard skin

In yet other instances the skin has been cut to produce a straight edged cape-like garment consisting simply of a rectangular piece of hide though it is not clear how this was held on or around the shoulders (figure 67). It is possible that such pieces were not in fact tailored skins but other material, linen or wool, decorated to imitate leopard skins. In at least one scene an 'overseer of linen' is shown carrying in such a tailored rectangular leopard skin garment. Note also the two imitation leopard skin vestments with applied gold 'spots' which were found in the tomb of Tutankhamun.

Less elaborate priestly robes consisted of the standard short kilt worn with a so-called lector priests' 'sash'. This was merely a piece of material about 5 to 8 cm wide worn diagonally across the chest and over one shoulder. In some examples it could be attached to the kilt itself part of which projected above the waistband at the back (figure 68). Although often referred to as the lector's sash it was not exclusive to lector priests and was often worn by others, not necessarily in connection with priestly duties.

The groups of mourning women who customarily accompanied the funeral procession wailing and weeping have been mentioned above. On its arrival at the cemetery or the tomb itself the coffin was greeted by ritual dancers called the Muu who wore tall hats, probably made of reed, not dissimilar to the White Crown in appearance (figure 69).

New Kingdom

Figures wearing the lector's sash or dressed in a leopard skin remain common throughout the New Kingdom. In most instances the leopard skin is worn in conjunction with a short kilt either plain or, later, pleated. The leopard skin garment is only worn by specialist priests such as the lector priest, a priest known as 'the pillar of his mother', another called 'son whom he loves' or the main priest officiating at a particular ceremony.

A peculiar variant of the leopard skin mantle is a garment, seemingly a dress, depicted on a figure of Queen Hatshepsut in her temple at Deir el-Bahri (figure 70). Here the fore paws of the skin are shown as if forming short sleeves whilst the hind paws lie side by side at the front hem of the dress an impossibly long distance from the front paws. The dress flares out widely from mid calf though there is a straight hem below the rear paws suggesting that a more conventional dress or skirt was worn underneath. Unfortunately the section of the temple in which the relief occurs is badly damaged and much detail has been lost. Assuming that we are not dealing with a case of ancient artistic licence it is possible that the mantle was not made from a real skin or that it was composed of several skins. The flare and the apparent stubbiness of the hind paws as portrayed would support the former. On the other hand the latter possibility receives support from the fact that the front feet retain claws. Yet a further possibility is that we are dealing with a manufactured garment to which only parts of the real animal have been attached parallel to the royal fashion of adding a bull's or giraffe's tail to the back of the belt or waistband.

An important officiant in the funeral ceremony was the *sem*-priest who

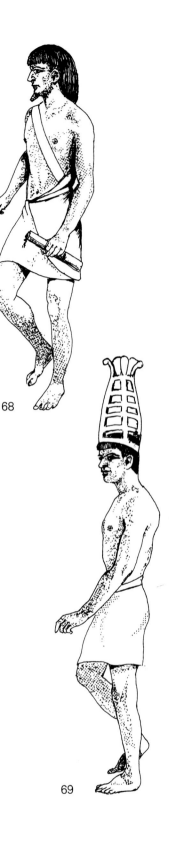

68

69

may have acted as a professional stand-in for the eldest son of the deceased who should in theory perform the burial rites for his father. At one point in the ceremony he is shown wearing a yellow striped, fairly full gown interpreted by some commentators as a bedgown (figure 71). Elsewhere in the proceedings he wears a reed cape over the back of his shoulders and tied across the front of his neck, perhaps as protection against a ritual beating (figure 72).

Another, more obscure specialist priest who took part in the funeral procession was called the 'great servant'. He wore a long cape-like mantle and carried a long baton, presumably connected with his office (figure 73).

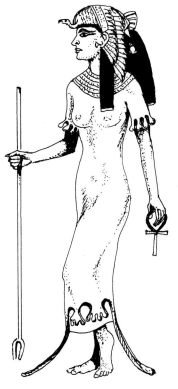

70

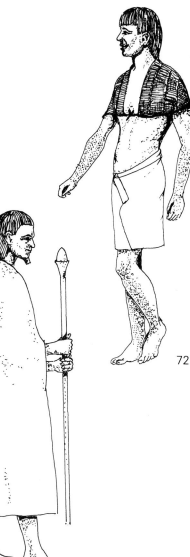

68　The so-called lector priest's sash

69　Muu dancers in their tall hats

70　Queen Hatshepsut in a variant of the leopard skin garment

71　A *sem*-priest in a yellow striped gown

72　A *sem*-priest wearing a reed cape

73　A 'great servant', one of many specialist priests

71

73

72

41

GODS

After mummies, pyramids, hieroglyphs and Tutankhamun one of the most lasting popular impressions of ancient Egypt is the bewildering number, literally several hundred, of gods which were worshipped. There was no single doctrine of faith in ancient Egypt and no essentially religious tome such as the Bible or the Koran. The afterlife was a belief not a faith and the Book of the Dead (more correctly the 'Chapters of Coming Forth by Day') was a manual of how to gain assured access to that afterlife; it was in no way equivalent or parallel to a Holy Book. The majority of Egyptian gods arose from some aspect of nature – animals or natural phenomena such as the sun, the moon, the weather, the desert, the river and so on. As a result and coupled with the fact that originally each village might have had its own god(s) many were restricted to quite small localized areas; only a very few had a wider currency. Indeed throughout Egyptian history the majority of gods remained of purely local significance being worshipped only in their village of origin. A very few were elevated into national status either because they were the local god of a particular king or because they held a significant position in the mythology or acquired a major role in the various rites and ceremonies. Obviously in a work of this size only the latter national gods can be considered though in the later periods many of the minor local gods were assimilated to or amalgamated with one of the major ones.

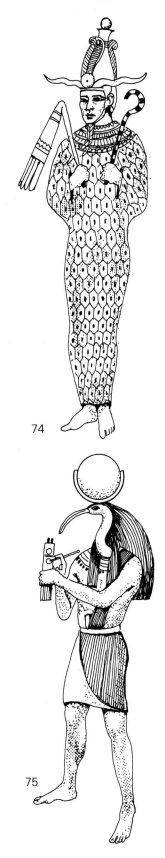

74

Although there are some costumes which are peculiar to the gods and not normally seen on mortals, divinities are generally distinguished and identified by the attributes, head-dresses and symbols with which they are adorned.

One of the most commonly encountered gods and perhaps the most important is the easiest to recognize. Osiris, originally a god of agriculture who as king of the underworld effectively became the god of the dead is appropriately enough normally shown mummiform, that is in the form of a mummy. As such he is totally enclosed in bandages or a linen shroud with only his two hands, laid across his chest, projecting (figure 74). In them he holds, as king of the underworld, the symbols of royalty, the crook and the flail. He normally wears the *atef*-crown, a composite head-dress consisting of the White Crown with uraeus flanked by ostrich feathers and often including a small sun disc on top as well as wavy ram's horns below. On some examples the shroud is decorated with a design of hexagons containing circles, scale patterns or rosettes, yet another emblem of royalty.

Many of the gods are shown in every day dress especially the ubiquitous kilt. Thoth for example, inventor of writing and scribe of the gods, is normally dressed as a lector priest with short semi-pleated kilt and the lector's sash (figure 75). He is often depicted in the act of writing and with the head of an ibis though the ape was also sacred to him.

Amun, chief of the gods during the New Kingdom, often wears a version of the archaic royal tunic with single shoulder strap marked by having a scale pattern all over it (figure 76). The belt and animal tail are familiar from

75

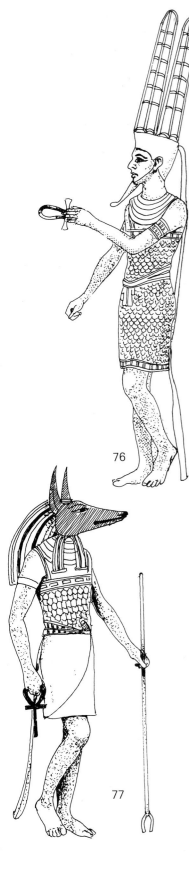

royal usage though the front flap is shorter than might be expected but retains the royal adjunct of uraeus serpents. This costume is in keeping with Amun's later role as king of gods. Elsewhere he is shown in the *shendyt*-kilt. His very characteristic head-dress comprises two tall plumes on a flat topped helmet. In his combined form with the sun god Re a sun's disc is usually added over the lower part of the plumes directly above the 'helmet'. Other gods are shown in a garment very similar to the archaic royal tunic but with two shoulder straps rather than one.

The jackal headed Anubis, god of embalming and the cemetery, wears a further variation of this in that his upper body is clad in a two strap tunic decorated with hexagons and a border of dots whilst below the belt the skirt appears to be of a wrap-around variety and was presumably a separate item (figure 77). The jet black head of Anubis is enough to pick him out of most scenes instantly without need for a head-dress.

Likewise, goddesses are most frequently seen in the every day sheath dress with two tapering shoulder straps and are marked out as divinities only by the headgear and symbols which identify them as such. In some examples the shoulder straps have rosettes applied at the point where they cross over the breasts. Generally speaking the gods seem to have shunned the more elaborate fashions introduced in the later New Kingdom with their crush of pleats. However the four goddesses who protect the wooden canopic shrine of Tutankhamun are an exception to this.

Unusual decoration occurs on some of the divine garments such as the illustration here of a divinity called Weret-Heka literally meaning 'Great of Magic'. The sheath dress has a double border of dots with scale pattern over the rest of it coming to a rounded point just above the knees. Two broad bands cross over on the waist and these are perhaps a development of the practice of depicting some goddesses with vultures' wings criss-crossing their garments (figure 78).

74   The god Osiris

75   Thoth, scribe of the gods, in lector priest's dress

76   Gods often wear a version of the archaic royal tunic decorated with a scale pattern; the god depicted here is Amun

77   Anubis, god of embalming

78   A goddess in a sheath dress

The only distinguishing mark of most deities is a distinctive attribute or symbol which unmistakingly identifies them as a particular god or goddess.

One of the most important of the Egyptian gods for example, at least from the fourth dynasty onwards, was Re, the sun god, who was head of the council of gods and the ultimate judge. His symbol, not surprisingly, is the sun's disc often combined with a uraeus to signify his power. All gods who made some sort of claim to superiority or universality above their local significance usually linked themselves to Re to form composite gods such as Amun-Re, Sobek-Re, Horus-Re, etc, as a result of which the sun's disc appears in the head-dresses of many gods.

The living king was associated with Horus a sky god and son of the god Osiris with whom the dead king was associated. The sacred animal of Horus was the falcon and so he is normally depicted with a falcon's head wearing the double crown of Egypt. Horus was thus an important god and not surprisingly he is found worshipped in several localities in slightly different forms and even as a national god he manifests himself in different guises. Some of the more important variations are Re-Horakhty, a combination of Re and Horus connected with the horizon, Haroeris or Horus the Elder, Harsiesis, Horus Son of Isis and, most frequent in the later periods Harpocrates or Horus the Child who is usually shown naked as was usual with children, wearing the side lock of youth and sometimes sucking his finger. The more fanciful depictions show him wearing a three plumed crown (figure 79).

The mother of Horus and wife of Osiris was Isis whose principal place of worship in the later periods of Egyptian history was her temple on the Island of Philae now raised from beneath the floodwaters of the Aswan dam. She was one of the four goddesses who protected coffins and mourned the dead. She is normally depicted standing in a long sheath dress with a head-dress in the form of the hieroglyph used to write her name, which probably represents some sort of seat (figure 80). However, bronze figures of the goddess often show her seated and suckling her child Horus; on such figures she normally wears a disc and horns head-dress (figure 81). Isis' sister Nephthys was another of the four goddesses who protected coffins and she likewise is shown as a woman in a long sheath dress with the hieroglyphic symbol representing her name, in this instance a basket on top of a sign showing a rectangular enclosure in plan (figure 82).

79   Harpocrates (or Horus-the-child) with a three-plumed crown

80   Isis wearing a headdress in the form of the heiroglyph used to write her name

81   Isis wearing the disc and horns headdress

82   The distinctive headdress of Nephthys represents the hieroglyph used to write her name

79

80

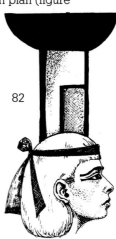

82

81

44

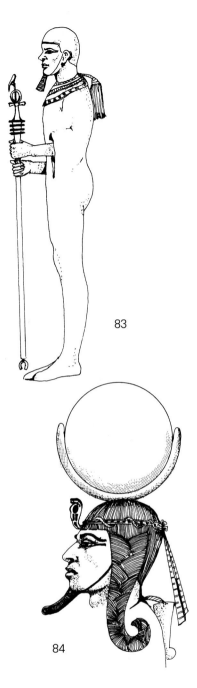

Another of the earliest of the Egyptian gods, Ptah, like Osiris is normally represented as a mummy. Ptah of Memphis was the main character in one of the Egyptian creation myths where he was thought first to have conceived the world before creating it, including the other gods and men, by his word. Unlike Osiris Ptah is usually bare headed, either bald or with closely cropped hair but sporting an artificial beard. Apart from his head only his hands emerge from the shroud and bandaging and in these he grasps a triple sceptre composed of a *was*-sceptre, a *djed*-pillar and an *ankh*-sign which respectively are based on the hieroglyphs for the words dominion, stability and life (figure 83). Another god who is often shown with the same triple staff is Khonsu, the moon god. He is normally depicted as a human with a head-dress consisting of a crescent and a disc (the latter representing the full moon rather than the sun) (figure 84).

Obviously it is not possible to give examples of all the divine symbols and attributes here and a few more will suffice to give an idea of general appearance. The goddess of truth, Ma'at, and the god of the air, Shu, are respectively shown as a woman and a man but both wear a single feather on their heads. Sobek was the crocodile god and normally appears with a crocodile's head sometimes wearing a head-dress of disc and plumes surmounting a pair of wavy horns from which uraei sprout (figure 85). Bastet, a cat goddess from the Delta, is depicted with a cat's head on a woman's body; she carries a sistrum and a basket in her hands (figure 86).

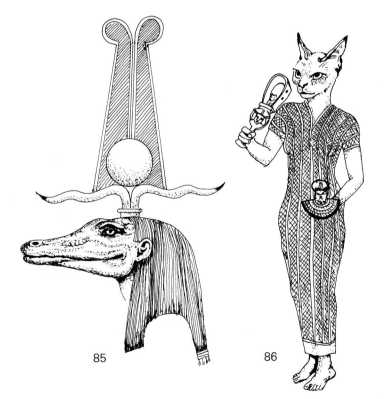

83   The god Ptah with his triple sceptre

84   The moon god Khonsu

85   The crocodile god Sobek

86   Bastet, a cat goddess, with sistrum and basket

7 Workmen and labourers

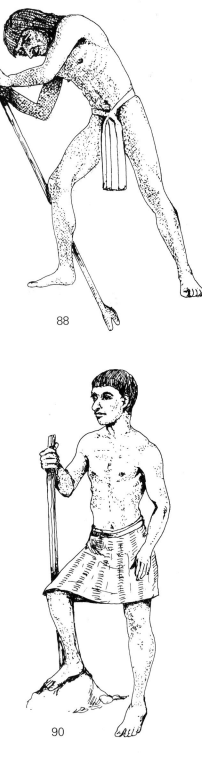

88

90

The Egyptian tomb scenes preserve for us an invaluable pictorial record of life in ancient Egypt. There is hardly a subject which does not appear somewhere amongst their rich variety. Commonest are agricultural scenes giving us an insight into ancient agriculture – ploughing, sowing, harvesting, threshing, winnowing, herding livestock. Other scenes record the more industrial side of life such as woodworking, metalworking, leather working, weaving and spinning – all the major crafts of Egypt. Yet others record details from the career of the tomb owner – the type of office which he held, his promotions, any special duties which he might have been called upon to perform. Elsewhere might be seen glimpses from the everyday life of the tomb owner showing him playing a board game, hunting or trapping in the marshes, at a banquet with dancers and musicians in attendance, simply sitting relaxing next to his pet animal and so on. In all of these there are invariably workmen, craftsmen, labourers, fieldworkers, servants, attendants, etc.

Old Kingdom

Male workers, especially agricultural employees, are often depicted totally naked; herdsmen driving cattle through water are almost always so. Very occasionally they wear a scarf, described as a stole, simply thrown around the back of their necks. Like the example shown in figure 7 these are also striped but appear to be somewhat longer perhaps merely due to the different method of wearing them.

In other scenes workmen are seen in a skimpier version of the kilt, somewhere between the true wrap-round kilt and a loincloth in appearance (figure 87). It is shorter than the short kilt worn by the nobles reaching only to about mid thigh length. It appears from the depictions to consist of a semi-circular piece of cloth or a piece of cloth cut to a curve at both sides which wraps around the buttocks and thighs and is secured by a belt. A rectangular flap of material is tucked through the belt and hangs down the front to cover the genitals. It is obvious from occasions where the wearer is bending over, allowing the front flap of material to fall forward, that no underwear was worn. It is likely that such garments were worn more for practicality than as a social distinction allowing as they would much greater freedom of movement in walking, bending and squatting as required by agricultural workers and artisans such as brickmakers and carpenters. Indeed more sedentary workers such as offering bearers,

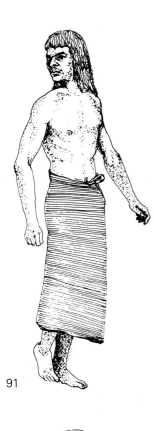

91

92

foremen and musicians often have a simple version of the nobles kilt though sometimes cut a little shorter.

Those workers engaged in netting or spearing fish and trapping birds in the marshes are normally shown in briefer garments still. This consists of little more than a linen belt with a triangular flap hanging from the front to cover the private parts (figure 88). They are always shown with vertical lines suggesting either that they were pleated or made up from separate thin strips of material. Some of the men wear it pulled up and tucked through their belts obviously to prevent it from flapping about.

Hunters after game or returning from the desert with their pack of dogs on leashes wear a knee length tunic of horizontally striped material. This is cut diagonally across the chest and ties over the left shoulder with a simple knot (figure 89).

Middle Kingdom

The workers of the Middle Kingdom continue on the whole to wear the same fashions as those we have described above. In addition one can mention a series of garments which it has been suggested were made of cane, straw or some similar material. They are always worn by herdsmen or people closely associated with cattle and come in three varieties: short kilts, long kilts and tunics. The short kilts (figure 90) are held up by a tied belt and project at the front as if starched. They are painted yellow and have thin vertical lines with diagonal hatching suggesting the twists of rope. It is largely on the basis of this that it has been assumed that they were made of straw, perhaps plaited, as linen is normally painted white in the tomb scenes despite the fact that unbleached or undyed linen would have been more of a yellowish buff colour. The longer versions extend to the mid calf (figure 91), are also supported by a knotted belt and likewise project quite stiffly at the front. They are always drawn with very close horizontal lines, perhaps indicating cane or rushwork. It is unlikely that peasant workers such as herdsmen would have had linen robes with fine horizontal pleating as might otherwise be the case here. Finally, rarest of all is a sleeveless tunic reaching to just below the knees and probably of the same material (figure 92).

87   See colour plate 2

88   Fisherman in a linen belt with triangular flap

89   See colour plate 2

90   A herdsman's kilt, possibly made of reed or straw

91   Longer version of the herdsman's kilt

92   Sleeveless tunic

In one tomb scene at el-Bersheh two attendants are depicted, both in simple short kilts and both carrying elaborate fly whisks; one also carries a long staff and the other a short one. The unusual feature of these two however which most concerns us here is that they have an oval 'plate' for want of a better word apparently strapped to their chests by fairly broad (5 to 8 cm) bands which cross in the centre of the plate to form an X and pass over both shoulders and around the back (figure 93). The men form part of a procession of bearers the leading figure of which brings in a large hide shield and the subsequent figures bows and bow cases so it is possible that the plates may have had a military use resembling as they do breast plates but this is not certain.

New Kingdom

In the New Kingdom the predominant garments of the working man remain the brief loincloth or the short kilt. The loincloths were made either of linen or, for the more physical professions such as brickmaking, of leather (figure 94). The example illustrated here is coloured brown in the original painting with black dashes perhaps indicating openwork decoration. Note that a patch on the seat, the area most likely to receive wear, was left without decoration. In at least one scene two men shown performing the same task wear respectively a loincloth and a short kilt suggesting that there was no particular social or rank distinction between the two garments. Presumably it was purely a matter of personal choice as to which one wore. Later in the New Kingdom the 'white collar' workers such as attendants are even seen in simple multi-pleated kilts.

A variety of other kilts or methods of wearing the traditional kilt are encountered on New Kingdom workers. One (figure 95) is similar to the Syrian and *Keftiu* kilt hanging as it does in a point at the front. Unlike the foreign counterparts however Egyptian examples are always devoid of decoration and are made of plain white linen. Farm workers in one scene exhibit three styles of kilt in use simultaneously by workers of apparently equal rank and status. One wears the simple kilt. A second figure has on a lightly pleated garment with a long rectangular piece hanging down the front and ending in a fringe (figure 96). Their companion's kilt is so draped as to form a long back apron over the buttocks descending well below the backs of the knees. The other end of the cloth is brought behind and over the waistband to hang down at the front and so cover the genitals but stopping short of the knees (figure 97). On some examples of this type of kilt the hem of the shorter front piece has a scalloped edge.

A herdsman with dishevelled hair from an eighteenth dynasty tomb wears a white linen tunic which recalls the Old Kingdom huntsman's cloak (see figure 89) by being crudely knotted over one shoulder.

Several specimens of real leather loincloths as described above have been preserved in ancient tombs. They were shaped as in figure 98. The wider section was placed over the buttocks and tied around the waist and the tongue shaped piece passed up between the legs and also tied around the waist. It is likely that a linen loincloth was worn beneath to prevent the

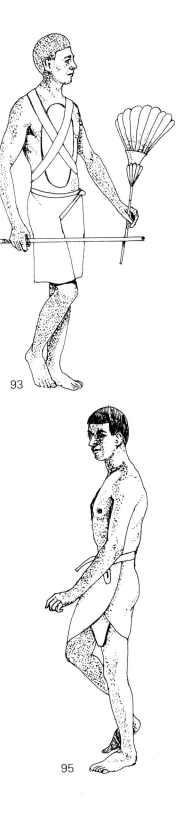

93

95

48

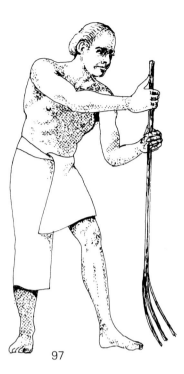

leather chafing against the skin especially with the rougher bull's hide examples. Such linen loincloths which could of course also be worn alone have been preserved in even greater numbers, one tomb having fifty of them. They take the form of inverted triangles with a concave base (figure 99) and were tied around the waist in similar fashion to the leather ones though it is possible that the front piece simply tucked through the waist ties coming from the back corners.

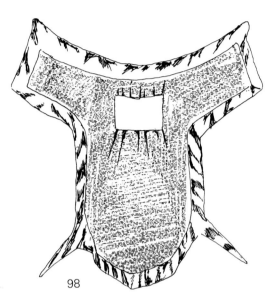

97

98

93   Attendant with oval 'breast plate'

94   See colour plate 7

95   Workman's kilt hanging in a point at the front

96   See colour plate 7

97   Kilt wrapped so as to form a long back apron

98   A leather loincloth

99   Triangular linen loincloth based on surviving examples

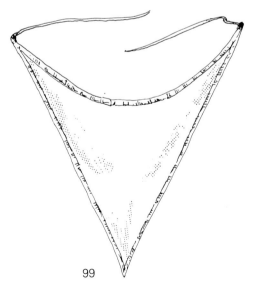

99

8 Military dress

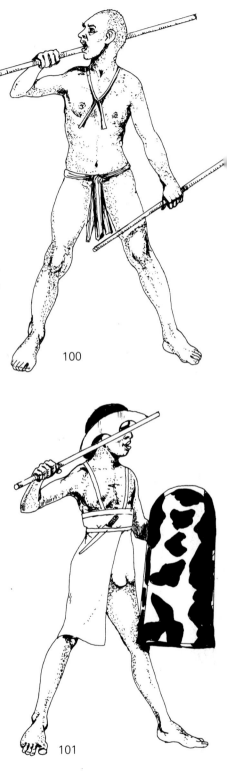

Egypt was, geographically speaking, a fairly isolated land with natural boundaries of desert and water between her and her neighbours which presented a formidable obstacle to any would be intruders. Nevertheless the earliest monuments record military activity though their exact interpretation is poorly understood. Depictions of battles in the Old Kingdom and Middle Kingdom sources are not common and they tell us little about the Egyptian army. The Old Kingdom texts speak of levies of troops on a local basis to meet specific needs though despite a lack of direct evidence some form of permanent force must have been maintained, if only as a royal body guard. During the Middle Kingdom evidence for a standing army is firmer but even so it was probably still quite small and local levies were still required for major operations. There is some evidence to suggest that the regular army was at least partially conscripted. It should be stated at this point that the Egyptian army was not merely a fighting force but was also called upon to carry out what may be termed economic exploration such as trading, mining and quarrying expeditions.

Because of her natural boundaries Egypt was only rarely attacked in a military sense from outside. During the New Kingdom however the strong pharaohs of the eighteenth and nineteenth dynasties adopted an aggressive foreign policy leading to the Egyptian 'empire' in Syria-Palestine. Regular campaigns were launched to hold existing or secure new territory in western Asia, largely to form a buffer state between Egypt and the other major near eastern powers – Hittites, Babylonians, Assyrians and Mitannians. To maintain these campaigns a large standing army was required, staffed by professional officers and soldiers. The army was divided into two wings – the chariotry and the infantry. Cavalry in the sense of mounted horsemen was not used. The chariotry was divided into squadrons of twenty five light two-wheeled chariots drawn by two horses. Each chariot had a driver with shield and a combatant armed with bow and arrow, spear(s) and sometimes a sword. Several categories of infantry are distinguished in the texts – the trained soldiers and veterans, the new recruits, special squads such as 'The Braves' (a royal crack unit) and 'shock-troops' and finally contingents of foreign mercenaries either volunteers, conscripts or drafted prisoners of war. Infantrymen might carry a combination of weapons selected from bow and arrows, axes, clubs, slings, spears and shield; they can generally be regarded as light infantry.

100

101

Old Kingdom

One of the rare depictions of soldiers from the Old Kingdom, in a fifth dynasty royal funerary temple, shows marines, or at least soldiers from the royal barge, carrying long wooden staves or bow cases. The troops wear a garment similar to that we have already seen on trappers in the marshes consisting simply of a belt or girdle around the waist with a triangular flap hanging from the front. Although in the former case there was some doubt as to whether this flap was a solid piece of material or separate strips of cloth there is no such doubt here. The soldier's garment was made of distinct strips (perhaps leather?) in this case three (figure 100). One of the figures wears a thin ribbon-like sash around his neck crossing on the chest but not attached to anything. They all have close cropped hair and wear no protection on their feet, upper body, arms or head. It is obvious therefore that their garments were for purposes of modesty rather than being protective. The officers and commanders wear a simple version of the official's kilt with a diagonally cut overlap.

Middle Kingdom

A small standing army of professional troops was maintained during the Middle Kingdom to man the royal and palace guards, to garrison the fortresses in Nubia and the Sinai border and to supervise the regular trading, mining and quarrying expeditions. The latter were manned largely by recruits raised through the local governors and although one instance is recorded of a force of ten thousand men most expeditions had only a few hundred members. On the whole they wore everyday dress such as simple kilts, occasionally with a triangular flap down the front, or a somewhat shortened version of the *shendyt*-kilt.

Other Middle Kingdom soldiers are shown wearing a long back apron which extends to at least the knees but is open at the waist to allow freedom of movement (figure 101). Under it they wear a variety of short kilts or loincloths, often with a shaggy or 'toothed' edge. In addition some have an arrangement of straps or webbing across their chests and around their backs presumably to support a quiver or some other piece of equipment. Others wear a tied head band often with a feather inserted in it perhaps as a regimental badge or as a sign of victory. Their only protection came from stout shields. These were rectangular with rounded tops and could be up to about five feet tall. They were made from hide with a leather edging strip sewn on separately and then attached to a wooden brace carved so as to form a hand grip. Archers wore leather wrist guards to protect them from the whip of the bowstring following release of the arrow (figure 102).

102

100   Soldier in a brief garment perhaps made of leather

101   Middle Kingdom soldiers in a long back apron

102   An archer's leather wrist guard

New Kingdom

Generally speaking the soldiers of the New Kingdom, as in previous periods, wore one of the varieties of short kilt with little or no other protection except possibly a shirt top. Coats of scale armour are however attested both in depictions and from surviving scales from the Middle Kingdom onwards. They do not become common until the New Kingdom and their introduction was perhaps largely due to western Asiatic influence. Certainly the lists of booty which Tuthmosis III took during his campaigns in Syria-Palestine included on one occasion 'one good bronze mail shirt of a chief and two hundred good bronze mail shirts of the army' as well as bronze helmets. Depictions of Egyptian armoured shirts show that they consisted simply of a sleeved bag-like tunic, similar to the many examples which have survived, to which were sewn elongated bronze scales (figure 103). The method of fastening the scales so that some flexibility was retained can be seen in figure 104 which is based on actual examples of scales. A leather collar was worn in conjunction with the armour to protect the neck with padded helmets, probably of leather rather than bronze, for the head. These often appear to have fringed edges and sometimes tassels from the top.

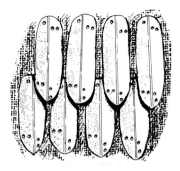

104

The foreign contingents of the New Kingdom army were basically the Nubians and the Sherden, one of the 'tribes' of the Sea Peoples (see below). In one tomb scene the raggy haired Nubian mercenaries are seen dressed in short linen garments combining the brevity and freedom of a loincloth with the modesty of a kilt. At the rear they have long net like aprons probably made from openwork leather. Black and white animals' tails are attached one to the back of the waist band and one to a garter-like strap around the knee (figure 105). The Sherden dress either in the native kilt of the Sea Peoples or in conventional Egyptian kilts. They can easily be distinguished however by their characteristic helmets which have curved horns sometimes with a disc on top (figure 106). They carry circular shields as opposed to the round-topped oblong shields of the Egyptians and wield heavy straight sided swords which taper to a point.

The principal enemies of the eighteenth dynasty kings were the people of Syria-Palestine, the Canaanites, whose dress is described below. In the nineteenth dynasty the Hittites became a threat with the notable but inconclusive battle of Kadesh in which Rameses II clashed with Muwatallis. The Egyptian reliefs show the Hittites wearing long Canaanite style tunics or armoured shirts rather than the short kilts which the native Hittite monuments reflect.

Rameses III of the twentieth dynasty (1198-1166 BC) has the distinction of fighting the first recorded combined sea and land battle during his repulsion of the attacks on Egypt by the Sea Peoples. The Sea Peoples were a loose confederation of tribes who originated from the Aegean islands of the Mediterranean. Their movements, which reached a peak during the twelfth century caused widespread destruction throughout the east Mediterranean. The best known group is the Philistines who subsequently settled on the coastal plain of Palestine which takes its name

105

103   See colour plate 8

104   Method of attaching armour scales

105   A Nubian mercenary

106

106 A Sherden mercenary in distinctive helmet

107 See colour plate 8

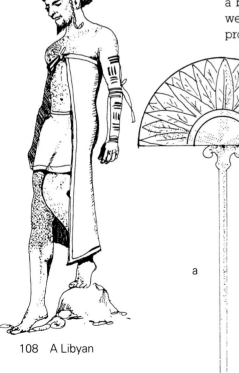

108 A Libyan

from them. The Sea Peoples wear kilts which very much call to mind those worn earlier by the *keftiu*. They also wear feathered head-dresses ornamented with decorative bands and tassels (figure 107). Like their brethren the Sherden they had circular shields and straight, tapering swords. Note that the Sherden mercenary contingent of the Egyptian army were actually fighting against their own people in the battles under Rameses III.

The other major clash during the reign of Rameses III was with the Libyans in the west. These people have a long, distinctive side lock on their otherwise coarse and straggly hair and carry a straight sword tapering to a point very much like that of the Sea Peoples but longer. Their dress consists of a cloak knotted over one shoulder and open down the front worn over a short plain kilt (figure 108). They have short pointed beards which are confined to their chins and appear much more goat-like than Semitic beards.

Military standards

Military standards in the form of emblems mounted on poles were apparently used in the earliest protohistoric periods. There is no evidence for them from the Old and Middle Kingdoms due to the paucity of military scenes but they become common in the New Kingdom with its increased military activity. The standards can be classified into three main types. Most frequent are fan-shaped standards (figure 108a) which in appearance are hardly distinguishable from the ostrich feather fans held by royal fan-bearers. However, they would probably have been made of wood with designs painted on them. A second variety consists of a square or rectangular device atop a pole, sometimes plain, sometimes with designs, sometimes with a feather attached (figure 108b). Finally a category of naval standards can be discerned the emblems of which are often in the form of a boat with a fan device over the cabin (figure 108c). All of these types were taken on to the field whereas other, more elaborate, standards were probably restricted to ceremonial use.

108a Fan-shaped military standard

108b Rectangular standard

108c A naval standard

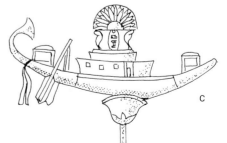

a

b

c

9 Foreigners

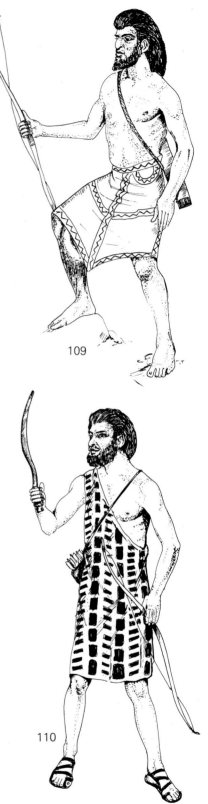

109

110

Egypt had had contacts with Syria-Palestine since late in the Old Kingdom and probably before that. Old Kingdom remains have been found at Byblos for example and it was probably customary for the Asiatic nomads to enter Egypt to pasture their flocks on the fringes of the Delta when the grazing in Palestine was exhausted. Increase in the numbers of Asiatics entering Egypt possibly helped to cause the economic stagnation and instability which brought about the end of the Old Kingdom. Asiatic immigrants in the twelfth dynasty became such a problem that king Amenemes I built a wall in the Delta region to keep them out. There were watch posts at regular intervals and reports on the movement of foreigners were kept. The earliest depiction of Asiatic nomads is in a tomb at Beni Hasan showing a small caravan of Asiatics herding donkeys, some of which are loaded with the eye paint used in great abundance by the Egyptians more as a preventative against various eye diseases than for cosmetic reasons. The men wear either skirts which fall to just below the knees and have fringed hems (figure 109) or tunics of a similar length which pass over one shoulder (figure 110). The women wear a garment identical to the men's tunic passing over only one shoulder but fitting tightly into the opposite armpit so that both breasts are covered (figure 111). Most of the men are wearing sandals made up of leather straps whilst the women go barefoot. All the garments, men's and women's, have brightly coloured geometric patterns on them. It is likely that they were made of wool rather than linen as this thread would have been more readily available to the nomads, probably indeed from their own flocks, and its extra warmth would have been required on cold desert evenings sleeping in a makeshift tent.

Contact was also maintained with desert dwellers to the west who, for want of a better term, are normally referred to as Libyans. They were marked as being foreign by their paler skins, red hair and blue eyes. They are often represented wearing feathers in their hair and phallus sheaths. Their thick hair often hangs in a long curl down one side of the head. They inhabited the marginal lands, which may well have been less arid than they are today, and the oases west of the Delta and the Nile valley as well as the strip along the Mediterranean coast. In the tombs at Beni Hasan the Libyans appear not dissimilar to the Asiatic nomads though their dress is different; the short pointed beards are as likely to be an indication of foreigners in general at this period than any observed ethnic difference.

111

The men wear short kilts stopping just above the knees made from cloth with simple geometric designs, mainly horizontal rows of zigzags (figure 112). A long thin flap hangs down the front apparently on the inside of the kilt. Yet others wear a long tunic though the details of this are not clear; it may have passed over both shoulders. The men in these fuller garments have much longer hair with feathers stuck in it. The Libyan women wear only a simply cut calf-length skirt with a 'crimped' hem. They have long hair turned up into a large curl at the end (figure 113). The men carry variously bows, axes, bent throwing sticks often erroneously referred to as boomerangs, and shields which differ in shape from Egyptian ones being rectangular with a V-shaped notch cut out of both ends.

Egypt's closest neighbours were the people of the south below the first cataract and from what is now the Sudan. Many Nubians actually lived and worked in Egypt mostly as servants or in the army. By the Middle Kingdom immigration had reached such a level that a series of fortresses was built in Nubia in order to monitor the flow of Nubians who were only allowed to pass if on genuine business and they had to return to Nubia after conducting that business. Papyri have survived which record the comings and goings at these fortresses. Nubia was important to Egypt as a rich source of gold and cattle as well as providing a tap into the luxury products of tropical Africa – leopard skins, elephant tusks, various spices, ostrich eggs and feathers to name but a few. The relatively lowly and perhaps 'exploited' nature of these people is best reflected in depictions of Beja herdsmen who are shown very emaciated with stick-like limbs and their ribs clearly visible beneath the flesh. They wear an extremely simple loincloth (figure 114) probably made of gazelle hide. Their hair is unkempt

112

109   A Middle Kingdom Asiatic skirt

110   A Middle Kingdom Asiatic tunic

111   An Asiatic woman of the Middle Kingdom

112   Libyan in a kilt with simple geometric decoration

113   Libyan woman

113

and their beards sparse and equally bedraggled; note the lack of moustache on the upper lip. The mark of their trade is a staff made from a crudely trimmed twig or branchlet. Obviously the Nubians who served in the army or as attendants to the richer families would have fared better and negro 'slave' girls are shown wearing close fitting calf-length skirts with geometric designs (figure 115). Other Nubian women wore leather skirts and actual examples of such garments have been recovered from several sites.

New Kingdom

Nubians

In the New Kingdom the most distinctive attire of the Nubians remained the scanty loincloth. These are often coloured with reddish-brown or black spots on a white ground suggesting that they were made of bull's hide. Actual examples of such leather loincloths have been found amongst the grave goods of some tombs usually however made of gazelle skin. They are cut in one piece and decorated with an openwork design consisting of horizontal rows of many small rectangular windows spaced so closely together that they give a lattice work, almost woven, effect. Other examples are decorated with cutwork designs. Such loincloths are found on Nubian workers, Nubians presenting tribute before pharaoh as well as on soldiers.

Elsewhere the Nubian tributaries are represented by the artists in simple Egyptian linen kilts or, later, in the pleated robes of the period with diaphanous skirts and keyhole necks. A less usual depiction of a Nubian chieftain shows him wearing a long pleated robe decorated with beadwork and other patterns. The robe is coloured blue with details in green though these may well be artistic convenience and probably do not represent exact colours (figure 116). Headgear often consisted of a feather or feathers pushed through a headband.

Depictions of Nubian women are not common and when employed as serving girls or dancers would have worn one of the costumes described in chapter 4. At least two scenes contain native Nubian women however, perhaps captives or women destined to enter service in the palace, in which they wear fairly loose fitting calf-length skirts, pleated and scalloped along the bottom hem (figure 117). They are held up by a triple strand belt or girdle and are mostly coloured bright red except for one example which has white spots on a black ground. The women carry their babies in deep hemispherical baskets which rest against their back and are supported by a thin strap passing across the front of their head just above the forehead. Children, as was customary throughout Egypt, went naked until they reached puberty.

Wealthier Nubian women wore Egyptianized clothes. One scene in the tomb of an official from the reign of Tutankhamun shows a Nubian princess wearing long pleated diaphanous robe typically worn by later New Kingdom Egyptian ladies.

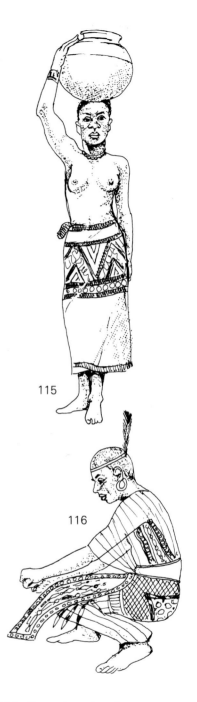

115

116

114   See colour plate 4

115   A Nubian serving girl of the Middle Kingdom

116   A Nubian chieftain

117

Puntites

Probably to be located on the Ethiopian or Somali coast Punt was visited by Egyptian expeditions from the late Old Kingdom onwards usually by boat down the Red Sea. It was noted for its exotic produce such as incense, gold, cynocephalous baboons and various resins and spices to such an extent that the Egyptians always spoke of the 'marvels' of Punt never merely the produce or tribute. The most famous expedition of all was that sent by Queen Hatshepsut which is recorded in considerable detail, both verbal and pictorial, on the walls of her mortuary temple at Deir el-Bahri. She even went so far as to have entire incense trees brought back with their root balls in basket work plant pots which were subsequently planted in the forecourt of her temple.

The Puntites are shown in kilts which have two curved pieces coming across the thighs and up to the waist band rather as on a *shendyt*-kilt. However in place of the central rectangular piece the Puntites have two long thin strips each of which tapers to a point. A ribbon hangs from the back of the belt though this may simply be the end of a tie (figure 118). They wear their hair either very closely cropped or shoulder length and they usually sport long thin beards. Not uncommonly a choker type necklace is worn around their necks made of spherical beads quite widely spaced apart.

The artist of Hatshepsut's temple in a rare glimpse of actual artistic observation has shown the steatopygous queen of Punt who is clad in a calf-length sleeveless dress with a plain straight hem and round neck (figure 119).

Other depictions of Puntites cannot be relied upon as accurate as they show a peculiar mixture of traits known to be associated with Syrians or Cypriots or the Mediterranean peoples in general.

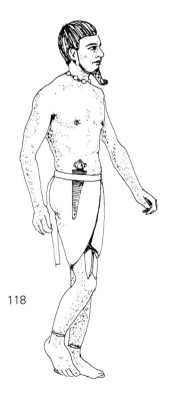

118

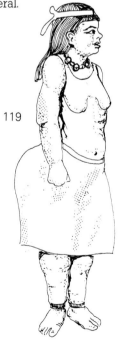

119

117   Captured Nubian woman in a calf length skirt

118   A Puntite kilt

119   The queen of Punt

Keftiu

Several Egyptian tombs of the New Kingdom contain a scene recording presentation of tribute to pharaoh and in some of these there is a distinctive group of people referred to as the *keftiu*. Scholars have for a long time debated the identity of these people who show some Minoan (ancient Cretan) features and it is now generally accepted that they represent the people of Crete. At any event they are certainly an east Mediterranean people.

Their dress is always a kilt and always quite distinctive by being decorated with intricate and busy designs composed of brightly coloured geometric patterns. The most common way of cutting the kilt resulted in it curving up over both thighs leaving one edge slightly longer and falling down the front. The end of this was usually cut square and occasionally fringed though examples which come to a point are found. On the whole their belts were equally elaborate (figure 120). Variants do occur such as straight hemmed skirts (figure 121) and some with more elaborate, tasselled decoration.

A slightly earlier depiction than those we have been considering seems to present an entirely different costume in that the kilt is cut away at the front such that it only covers the buttocks and backs of the thighs. At the front a long cod piece is worn (figure 122). It has been suggested that this may represent an earlier style of *keftiu* fashion or, less likely, that cod pieces and back aprons were worn under the conventional kilt. The main evidence for the latter hypothesis is that in one tomb the artist had originally drawn the *keftiu* with such cod pieces but these were painted out and replaced by the kilts described above.

A much rarer *keftiu* garment was made from the skin or skins of an animal which, to judge by the indication of claws, was probably a feline of some sort though it appears to have had a bushy tail (figure 123). The men wearing these garments appear as part of the rank and file offering bearers and do not seem to have held any special or privileged position which gave them priority over other members of the delegation.

On their feet the *keftiu* wear, if anything, an open-toed sandal but with heels and side pieces which extend almost to the toes and thus in effect almost a light shoe. With them they wear what is assumed to be socks also decorated with geometric designs. In many cases these appear to be multiple anklets but a few figures preserve designs on the instep and on top of the foot making some form of hose a more likely interpretation. Of course it is not impossible that anklets were also worn.

Above all else it is their hair which is particularly characteristic of the *keftiu* all of whom have two long thin wavy rat's tails hanging down their backs almost to waist level. Some figures have additional side locks which fall in distinct clumps and curl over at the ends. Most of them also have one, two or three backward curls on the front part of their crowns. The *keftiu* are always clean shaven and sport neither moustaches nor beards.

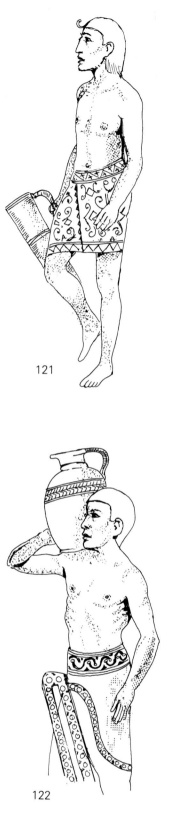

121

122

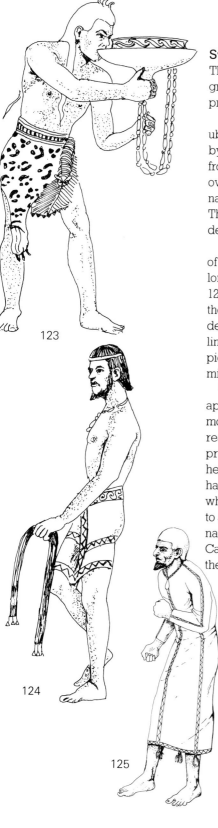

Syrians

The Syrians (perhaps more correctly Canaanites) are another distinctive group of foreigners quite often represented in the scenes showing the presentation of tribute.

Four main garments can be discerned for the Canaanite men. Firstly the ubiquitous kilt (figure 124) which in this case is very similar to the kilts worn by the *keftiu* in that it curves up over the legs and hangs in a point at the front. The major difference is that the Canaanite ones rarely have the all-over decoration found on the *keftiu* kilts; instead they are decorated with narrow bands usually forming borders but also running across the fabric. These borders are normally decorated with zigzags or some other simple device in red or blue. This type is used throughout the New Kingdom.

In the earlier part of the eighteenth dynasty up to and including the reign of Amenophis II (1413 BC) the commonest Canaanite garment consists of a long sleeved tunic reaching either to mid calf length or the ankles (figure 125). It has a keyhole neck held closed by ties with tassels on the end and the hem often has a few tassels hanging from it in line with the bands of decoration. These garments are always white and presumably therefore of linen. Narrow borders and bands are decorated with zigzags or dots picked out in red or blue or a combination. Such tunics very much call to mind the modern Egyptian *galabiyeh*.

There is a difference in Canaanite hairstyles on the tomb scenes which appears to be linked to costume though it may ultimately prove to be little more than artistic convention. The men in kilts usually have long hair reaching to or just above their shoulders flaring out at the back and producing a concave profile. It is held back out of the eyes by a simple headband. In contrast those in tunics normally have very closely cropped hair and no headbands. A very few Canaanites, all in tunics, have red hair which radiates from the crown of the head in fairly coarse strands and cut to an equal length all over (figure 126). Again it is held in place by a simple narrow headband and has a rather thatch-like appearance. All the Canaanites have short pointed beards and this is the characteristic mark of the Semite in Egyptian depictions.

120 See colour plate 5

121 A straight hemmed *Keftiu* kilt

122 An earlier style of *Keftiu* dress

123 A *Keftiu* garment made from an animal skin

124 A Canaanite kilt

125 A Canaanite long sleeved tunic

126 A less usual Canaanite hairstyle

After the reign of Amenophis II two other garments make an appearance. The first of these (figure 127) is really only a variation on the earlier tunic which remains unaltered but in use is embellished by the addition of a separate sash-like piece of cloth which is wrapped around the body roughly from the waist to the knees. This, like the tunic itself, has decorated borders.

The second of the new garments which remained in use at least until the end of the twentieth dynasty consists of a long garment probably made from a single square or rectangle of cloth wrapped around the body so as to fall in tiers. Over the shoulders is worn a separate cape in matching fabric reaching to about the middle of the back (figure 128). The material from which these garments are made is usually coloured with an all over red, blue or yellow ground with contrasting designs of rosettes, spots and so on in blue, red, green or white. Not uncommonly a contrasting or a negative border was used.

Canaanite women have very distinctive dresses coloured white in the tomb scenes, again probably made of linen (figure 129). They have a manufactured appearance falling as they do in overlapping flounces with a coloured fringe along the bottom of each flounce. Like men's tunics they vary from calf- to ankle-length. The dresses had very short sleeves but these are rarely seen as it was normal practice to wear a cape over their shoulders, even in the earlier part of the eighteenth dynasty, extensive enough to hide the whole of their arms. The bodice of the dress was given shape by means of a long coloured strap which passed around the back of the waist, crossed just below the breasts, passed over the shoulders and tied behind the neck leaving the tasselled ends hanging down the back. Their children generally went naked though in rare instances, perhaps sons of chieftains, wore miniature versions of the adult costume.

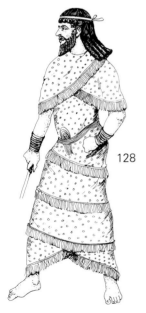

127

129

128

127 Tunic with band of material wrapped around

128 Later Canaanite wrap with a shoulder cape

129 Canaanite woman's flounced dress

10   Hair and wigs

130a

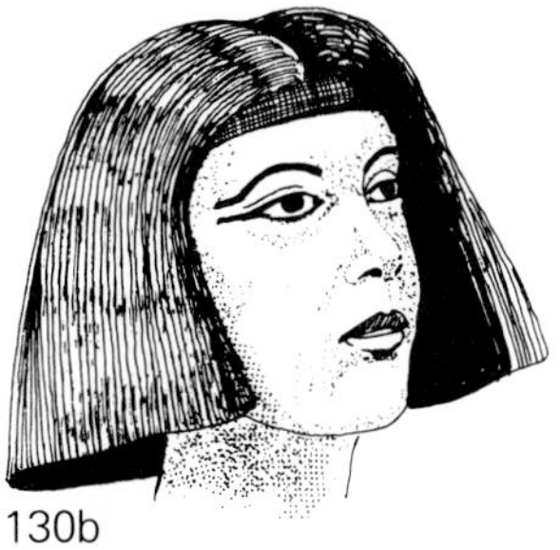

130b

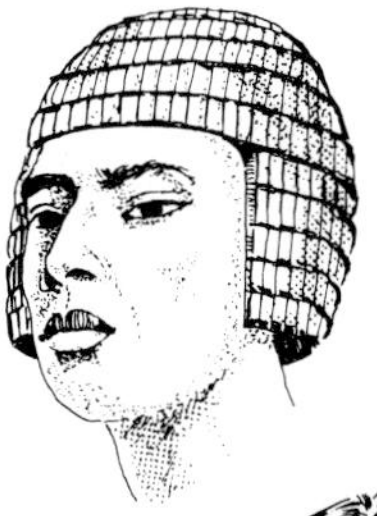

131

132

130   Old Kingdom bobbed wigs —
(a) man's, (b) woman's

131   An exclusively male Old
Kingdom wig

132   An early version of the lappet
wig worn by queens and goddesses
in the Old Kingdom

There is evidence from the earliest times that the Egyptians either shaved their heads or cut their hair very short. Children usually have very short hair or shaved heads except for a single long 'sidelock of youth' which hangs down one side of their head and curls over at the end. Women also often cropped their hair though dancers, singers and woman servants often have long natural hair. Both sexes left their hair to grow as a sign of mourning. It was quite normal for the upper classes to wear wigs made from human hair and these would have provided protection against the heat yet would probably have been cooler than their own hair. Men were normally clean shaven but the king and priests wore artificial beards on ceremonial occasions.

Old Kingdom
One of the most popular Old Kingdom wigs was worn by both men and women. This was a fairly full wig, bobbed at the shoulders or just above and with a central parting from which the hair was combed straight over the sides of the head. In the case of men the hair is swept back over the ears (figure 130a) whilst women's wigs are normally pulled in at the temple and then flare forward onto the cheeks (figure 130b).

An exclusively male wig was made up of overlapping tiers of short locks or chunks of hair cut square at the end (figure 131). They are usually close fitting and look rather like a cap. There is no parting and the hair forms a straight fringe across the forehead and falls down the sides of the head covering the ears completely. The back is cut square at collar or shoulder length.

Queens and goddesses in the Old Kingdom wear an early version of lappet wig, a long wig with central parting. The hair is combed so that it falls in two lappets which are brought over the front of the shoulders and another which hangs down the back (figure 132). The hair is pulled back behind the ears which are fully exposed.

Women with naturally long hair kept it in place with a single headband or ribbon.

Middle Kingdom
In the Middle Kingdom the man's version of the bobbed wig was replaced by a slightly modified style which lacked the central parting and tended to be at least shoulder length (figure 133). A new introduction, derived from

this and particularly characteristic of the twelfth dynasty, has two broad lappets which fall over the front of the shoulders and taper to a point towards the centre of the chest (figure 134). The hair is always pulled back behind the ears on such wigs and is often wavy with ringlets at the ends.

Women continue to wear the lappet wig alongside a more intricate one obviously derived from it. In this the wig is parted at both sides over the nape of the neck to leave a central pony tail hanging down the back which is usually cut square (figure 135). The two thicker side pieces are brought forward over the shoulders and their tapered ends are wound around disc-shaped ornaments into a spiral. Ribbons were used to hold the bunches and partings in place.

New Kingdom

There is more variety in hair styles during the New Kingdom as can be seen from the illustrations throughout the text. The tripartite lappet wig remains current especially for deities and sometimes women. A headband is often worn with it which ties at the back leaving the two ends dangling; the bunches of hair were often tied with bands as well.

Otherwise women wore a full heavy wig falling to an even length all round usually to the top of the breasts. These are invariably very elaborately worked into bunches, curls, ringlets or plaits often secured by ostentatious headbands (figure 136).

The normal style for men was the duplex wig (figure 137) which has the appearance of one wig superimposed on another because of the way the two pieces which fall over the front of the shoulders are worked in a different manner to the rest of the wig.

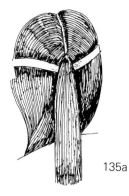

Accessories

That the Egyptians took their coiffure seriously can be intimated from the occurrence of hairdressing scenes in the tombs and the mention of barbers in the texts. In addition a variety of hair accessories can be seen in museums. Amongst these may be mentioned wood or bone combs, decorative pins, hair-rings in various materials (glass, gold, semi-precious stones), bronze hair curlers, razors and tweezers. Medical texts include recipes for lotions and applications which were used for treatment of scalp disorders and other hair problems.

133 Middle Kingdom version of the man's bobbed wig

134 A new form of wig introduced in the Middle Kingdom

135 Intricately coiffured woman's wig

Conclusion

In the later periods of Egyptian history New Kingdom fashions tended to continue. During the twenty sixth dynasty there was a revival of Old Kingdom styles for example in sculpture though this was merely a decadence which arose from thoughts of past glory and certainly does not reflect such a change in real garments of the time. During the Graeco-Roman period Greek and Roman fashions could no doubt have been seen in Egypt but it is likely that the simple native tunic continued as the basic garment for the mass of the population. That this was so is suggested by later Coptic textiles from the Christian era in Egypt whose simple T-shaped shirts are very reminiscent of earlier tunics. Coptic textiles have survived in vast quantities and many works have been devoted to them. Some of these are listed in the bibliography which follows.

136

Bibliography

Few works have been devoted to ancient Egyptian costume and the few that do exist are mostly specialist articles in learned journals which are very difficult to obtain. Those wishing to gain a better idea of ancient Egypt in general or the styles and variety of costume, colours, etc, can consult the many excellent and inexpensive popular books which are now available on subjects such as painting and sculpture.

HALL, R, *Egyptian Textiles: Shire Egyptology*, No. 4, Aylesbury 1986
HOUSTON, M G, *Ancient Egyptian, Mesopotamian and Persian Costume and Decoration*, London 1954

Coptic textiles
Again many specialized works exist but these are difficult to obtain. The three listed below contain further bibliographies:

KENDRICK, A F, *Catalogue of Textiles from Burying-Grounds in Egypt* volumes I-III, London 1920-22
SEAGROATT, M, *Coptic Weaves*, Liverpool 1965. A short but excellent introduction to the subject
START, L E, *Coptic Cloths*, Halifax 1914

137

136   A full, heavy New Kingdom wig

137   The New Kingdom man's duplex wig

Index